ZAO FAN
Breakfast of China

Dedicated to
MY GRANDFATHER, ZEE PAO SAN

ZAO FAN

Breakfast of China

WRITTEN AND PHOTOGRAPHED BY
MICHAEL ZEE
徐寶山

Interlink Books

An imprint of Interlink Publishing Group, Inc.
Northampton, Massachusetts

Zao Fan: Breakfast of China

There is something remarkably unpretentious about breakfast. Despite the well-known phrase, it is often considered the least important meal of the day, even within the spectrum of Chinese cooking, where lunch and dinner represent exquisite banquets, the artistry of chefs, and years of skill and training. Many breakfast stalls, on the other hand, prepare just one dish or a few bites for a tiny sum of money.

When I first visited China, it wasn't the diversity of the food that surprised me but the enormous availability, at all times of day, on every street and every corner. There is food absolutely everywhere. It may sometimes feel that many of the historic markets, which sell raw ingredients through a cooperative model, have given way to Western-style mall food courts or delivery apps, but I still see the old markets sitting alongside and even embracing the new. There is a never-ending stream of new ideas and reworked classics that add texture and diversity to the conversation.

The sheer enormity, complexity, and extensive history of Chinese food immediately turn any conversation about it into a philosophical study of the sublime. The vastness is both terrific and terrifying. What academic study of Chinese cuisine can provide in terms of historical insight, however, is often greatly removed from today's lived experience and what we put in our mouths. To paraphrase Confucius: everyone eats, but few truly understand the pleasure of taste.

For every living generation of Chinese people, so much will have changed in society since they were born, but on each street the same everyday encounter still takes place: a quick breakfast on the corner that is inexpensive, humble, and dependable. If we consider the country a vast tapestry of flavor, texture, and processes, then the meal of breakfast is an elemental thread in a story that is still being woven.

Today, the overwhelming majority of Chinese people eat breakfast out of the home. In major cities, high population density and shared accommodation meant that until recently many didn't have a private kitchen at home. In Shanghai, a *jianbing* (煎饼), a delicious savory pancake from the city of Tianjin, costs roughly 7RMB (around $1). This will be even less in smaller cities and towns. Hole-in-the-wall shops or noodle restaurants are staffed by a single person or a husband-and-wife team that are specialized in (or famous for) a single dish. Ordering takeout through apps like Meituan or Eleme is so easy and affordable that even I have been guilty of ordering breakfast from across the road rather than getting dressed and going out.

Zao Fan: Breakfast of China

At breakfast stalls and shops in China, barely is anything done by machine—machinery is impersonal and robs the sellers of their pride. With *jianbing*, for example, each vendor wants to differentiate themselves from the next. Their skillful handwork and the tools of their trade, like a carpenter or a cobbler, are marks of distinction and symbols of mutual validation. This is not a book about factory-made croissants or industrially farmed coffee—breakfast in China is about people making food to order, every day, sometimes just to glean a small existence.

Every province, village, and store will offer exciting variations of beloved dishes that follow certain defining characteristics. There are formal, historical classifications around what we might consider "elevated" regional cooking. Chinese cuisine is divided into eight broad styles, known as *bada caixi* (八大菜系) or the Eight Great Traditions. These are *yue cai* (粤菜) from Guangdong, *chuan cai* (川菜) from Sichuan, *lu cai* (鲁菜) from Shandong, *hui cai* (徽菜) from Anhui, *min cai* (闽菜) from Fujian, *huaiyangcai* (淮扬菜) from Jiangsu, *xiangcai* (湘菜) from Hunan, and *zhecai* (浙菜) from Zhejiang.

A region like Sichuan is most notably characterized by the use of chile and numbing pepper, a combination called *mala* (麻辣). This is just one of 24 detailed flavors in Sichuan cuisine, with one of my favorite, lesser known combinations being *guaiwei* (怪味), which translates as "strange flavor"—a mix of the numbing, spicy *mala* and *yuxiang* (鱼香), or "fish fragrance" (which ironically doesn't contain fish). Sichuan's neighboring province, Hunan, uses less of the numbing pepper and a greater intensity of heat. Wedged in the middle there is the mega-metropolis of Chongqing, now a distinct entity from its mother province of Sichuan, which has become a hotbed of wild experimentation in trends.

The localized cuisine of Shanghai is one of the sweetest, with an emphasis on condiments and pickles to enhance other ingredients, while the Cantonese cooking of Guangdong often maintains the integrity of terroir through cooking techniques like steaming and blanching and a careful use of spice, sugar, and salt. You will often hear the phrase *qingdan* (清淡) used to describe the light, delicate, and non-greasy qualities of Cantonese cooking, which to some palates can border on bland.

The enormous province of Xinjiang is one sixth of the landmass of China, a mix of Muslim and nomadic communities that include the Kazakhs, Xibo, and Tibetans to name a few. Its breakfast culture is full of tandoor-baked breads, lamb meat, and fermented dairy, and it is one of the few regions that almost never uses soy sauce. Xinjiang cuisine also includes bright, cold salad dishes that contrast with other rich and pungent dishes.

Yunnan, which is not part of the eight traditional cuisines of China, is made up of over 30 ethnic groups, with influences from neighboring Myanmar, Laos, and Vietnam. Its Eden-like weather and diverse terroir allows for the cultivation of everything from wine, mushrooms, coffee, and tea, to an incredible diversity of fruits and vegetables.

8

In recent years, it has felt like every new restaurant or natural wine bar in Shanghai is serving some interpretation of Yunnanese food. The breakfast foods from this province are some of my personal favorites.

A typical breakfast menu in China is more than an assortment of delicious food; it reads like a chronicle of over 4,000 years of history. From preserved millet noodles found in tombs (see page 144) to the daily necessities of life documented by a bureaucrat in exile during the Song Dynasty (see page 18), we can witness the ancient stories that have been written into these dishes. The Chinese are arguably the most food-orientated people in the world, with food impacting everything from language and customs to rituals and behavior.

The agricultural conditions of a province also influence its cuisine, perhaps most famously in the somewhat nebulous wheat and rice divide that separates northern and southern China. Whether cultures are nomadic, raise livestock, or plant crops, the stability or scarcity of food production dictates whether a cook will conjure up a steamer of finely pleated *xiao long bao* or a roughly chopped sandwich filled with donkey meat. Beijingers in the north, for example, fold and bake deliciously flaky *shaobing* breads with a mastery of gluten and crumb, whereas in Shunde, in the south, you're more likely to find a plate of steamed rice flour *changfen* with a velvety slipperiness that is almost impossible to pick up with chopsticks.

Everyone I know in China has an opinion on the food of other provinces, but there are certainly regions that are more popular than others and therefore more commercially viable, for example Cantonese. Dim sum was originally conceived in Guangdong as a simple snack of two bites to have with a cup of tea—a light meal suitable for every day. Over the twentieth century in Hong Kong, however, that slowly evolved into a long meal filled with pomp and ceremony. While it is certainly a very enjoyable experience, it also encourages us to spend more. This is a prime demonstration of the way in which capitalist market forces have become the creative engine behind changes in the Chinese diet.

The country is on track to become the largest consumer of coffee in the world by 2030, a trend that has grown alongside China's urban development and rapidly industrializing lifestyles, growing commuter culture, and the annual return of millions of students who have studied overseas. The practices of thousands of years of tea culture—in terms of cultivation, preparation, and consumption—have been poured into something new yet very familiar. Few cultures prize non-alcoholic beverages like the Chinese prize tea, which may be another reason that coffee culture has been able to boom in the way that is has. It could also be argued that there was a time when a sort of aspirational internationalism drove trends, but the Chinese have never had a taste for chocolate, despite many attempts at localization over several decades.

This eager embracing of new foods is nothing new, though. There is a long history of culinary influence and new ingredients coming to China from both near and far. Five hundred years ago, ingredients from the Americas like tomatoes, chiles, and potatoes supercharged the diets of the Old World, leaving a redefined food landscape. From my experience, the idea that innovation and tradition are mutually exclusive does not exist. Unlike Western countries that have mandated recipes stored in government archives (for example in Italy, where Bolognese ragu and Neapolitan pizza are protected from change rather than preserved for posterity), Chinese cooking is fluid and flexible. Recipes like Jidan Hanbao (page 209) and Yuni Bing (page 140) are a response to a demand in the market for new products that are still identifiably Chinese in character but which offer innovation. However, this flexibility also has its drawbacks, as very quickly gimmicks and trends can take over and an infinite plurality of options starts to make simple experiences frustrating. There was a momentary experiment with adding all sorts of chips and convenience store snacks to jianbing. While these fads do not always influence cuisine for the better, we should remember that food and culture exist in a moment of time, and unless we record what is happening, the flavor of the time and these micro-realities of taste will disappear.

Nostalgia is a powerful marketing trend everywhere, and over the last decade China has seen a surge in interest in pre-revolutionary recipes, retro-style restaurant interiors, and influencers like Li Ziqi and Dianxi Xiaoge, who create videos of their simple—if somewhat romanticized—life, making their own clothes and cooking with grandma in the countryside. It is now not uncommon for restaurants or coffee shops to open with the look and feel of 1960s colonial Hong Kong or a 1990s domestic setting like a living room or kitchen.

During one of the many conversations I had with my friend and chef Peiran Gong while writing this book, I asked her about her childhood in Dongbei, Northeast China. The harsh winters meant breakfast was usually eaten at home. In addition to the standard northern fare of fresh tofu with pickles and a starchy savory broth, she recalled that her family would eat sea cucumbers with honey, a combination that she found disgusting, preferring to chop them up and mix them with soy sauce and wasabi. She also fondly remembers drinking malted milk, *mai ru jing* (麦乳精), and one brand in particular, called Lacovo. This instant malty drink arrived in China in the 1930s and, over the decades, became a popular breakfast for growing children because of its ease of preparation, perceived health benefits, and inexpensive cost. In the 1990s it fell out of fashion, only to reappear again a few years ago in bubble teas and cakes flavored with a nostalgic twist.

What the future holds for Chinese food as it progresses through the circular nature of capitalist trends, notions of authenticity, and cultural identity (as well as the influences of returning international diaspora) is unclear, but whatever changes do take place will only continue to add to the cuisine's rich tapestry of flavor.

The journey to Zao Fan

In 2021, while researching this book, I found myself in Wuhan at a small restaurant—notably "the second best *re gan mian* shop" in town according to Dianping, China's most popular restaurant review app—which was owned by Mr. and Mrs. Yuan. Their shop was at the center of the community. Mr. Yuan told me how they were organizing medicine and food deliveries for their vulnerable neighbors during the Covid-19 pandemic, aware of the potential dangers. He was worried for the future and how the people of Wuhan would be affected. He asked me: "What will the world think of us?" Then, with a sigh, he looked at his wife and smiled. "We were so beautiful when we were young," he mused, "but this job makes you old."

I found a similar story when I visited a couple in Shanghai who were cooking delicious Huangshan-style rice near the neighborhood of Laoximen (see page 162). They said they knew their business would close after they died, having no children of their own to leave it to. Even if they had had children, they wouldn't want them to work like they do.

It made me think of a great deal about my own family, myself a third-generation Chinese cook who ultimately decided not to continue in the family business.

12 I was very young when my grandfather, Pao San, died. My Auntie Pauline sent me wonderfully long and detailed memories of what he was like. He was entrepreneurial, with a zest for life, and was a generous boss who would drive his staff home after late shifts. He was a perfectionist who demanded the same from everyone around him. I remember him sitting on the edge of a single bed in the living room, too frail to go upstairs. He had no idea when his exact birthday was, but he was born sometime around the start of the First World War on Zhoushan Island. I first visited my family shrine there in 2009. It is a serene spot, hidden among yangmei trees, the fruits of which are a wonderful delicacy with a terribly short season. It used to be a long drive and then a ferry to reach the island, but today a high-speed train and taxi will get you there in a fraction of the time.

Pao San was only a teenager when he moved to Shanghai to find work, and he soon found himself on a ship to Liverpool with the Blue Funnel Line, luckily escaping the city before the start of the Battle of Shanghai. He survived being torpedoed twice during the Second World War, despite the fact he couldn't swim. He returned to Shanghai to visit his parents and siblings just months before the formation of the People's Republic of China, then left one final time in 1949 and died in Liverpool in 1989, never to see his homeland or his parents again. When I moved to the magical city of Shanghai in 2017, I would walk the streets wondering where exactly my grandfather had lived, what his days were like, where he socialized, worked, and ate before his life as he knew it was turned upside down.

Zao Fan: Breakfast of China

In the 1950s, he started a small restaurant empire in Liverpool. First was the Empress Café opposite Lime Street Station, followed by the New World restaurant on Whitechapel, then The Bamboo in Crosby with various chip shops across the city, all of which served some sort of Anglo-Chinese fusion for the local market. He wasn't a superstar chef, never hosted exquisite banquets or wrote cookbooks, and will probably never be remembered in poetry or song, but he had fiercely loyal customers and staff that worked for him for decades. I only have fond memories of him from my childhood: a few photos and a menu from The Bamboo.

I remember Sundays spent with him in Liverpool's Chinatown, the oldest Shanghainese community in Europe. The city used to be so filthy and dark before its spectacular regeneration, which simultaneously erased so much of its grit and nuance. On Seel Street there was a Georgian townhouse with a Chinese café in the front room where they would sell *baozi* from what felt like enormous steamers. As a child, everything feels enormous, so I wish I had photographs of this place.

By the time I was living in Shanghai, I had already been posting every day to my Instagram account, SymmetryBreakfast, for five years, and the move further propelled me into exploring and researching the breakfast foods of China. From typical street foods, home-cooked leftovers, and government-provided quarantine breakfasts to meals experienced in the homes of poets, halfway up a holy mountain, at a vineyard, inside a restricted military zone, on trains, planes, and boats, I have eaten and documented so much, from the ordinary to the absurd.

14

I got my first film camera at the age of seven or eight and photography has been part of my life ever since. I am fortunate to have a father who was interested enough to have a black and white darkroom at home. I took photos of my lunch and dinner on 35mm film long before I had a mobile phone. I studied photography at university and am lucky enough to make a living from something that some just see as pressing a button. For me, a photograph is more than just an aide-mémoire or a snapshot of a fleeting moment. It is an extension of my vision and experience manifested into a tangible frame for others to witness, too. I wanted this book to be not just my voice, but also my sight.

That's why I have included QR codes with the recipes. Scanning one of these with your phone camera will transport you into my shoes as I watched these dishes being made, observing hands kneading dough or a bubbling pan of oil. Not every process was on show, but I did make my way into many kitchens. There is a great deal of transparency and visibility early in the mornings and the amount of knowledge I gained from simply watching the experts rather than reading is amazing. Through these videos, you will be able to see what I saw: the speed of the hand, what I really mean by "golden brown," how big that "handful" or "big pinch" really are. You can also catch glimpses of cultures and techniques that may cease to exist in the next century. In one video, you will see the father of my friend, Atina, singing in Xibonese about the Ili River that flows through the city of Yining on China's western border with Kazakhstan. It was a moment that made my heart soar. You can view all the videos on the dedicated *Zao Fan* website: zaofancookbook.com.

I have tried to write the recipes for a Western kitchen to the best of my abilities. Unfortunately, some variables might not be in your favor, for example how a Chinese tandoor will almost certainly exceed the heat of a domestic appliance, how the gluten structure of flours might differ, or how you might be reluctant to pay a premium for an ingredient that in China costs nothing. These are barriers I cannot always remove, but I have tried to think of workarounds or alternatives.

This book is a culmination of three important parts of my life: my love of breakfast and food, my love of China, and my love of photography, all mixed with my desire to break down barriers, to teach and to share in a way that is accessible and enjoyable. This is not an encyclopedia of breakfast in China and the aim of this book is not to be a complete academic overview.

Ultimately, I want you to use this book as a multi-functional tool. Take it as a jumping off point to perhaps one day go and visit these people in the photos and taste their food for real (they are wonderfully friendly and kind cooks and hosts). Use it as an enhanced instruction manual to bridge the gap in knowledge between descriptor and practice, the word and the hand. Or, read it as pure entertainment—just sit in an armchair and explore one of the greatest cuisines in the world, through the greatest meal of the day.

15

Sunrise over the karst mountains of Guilin, Guangxi province.

Zao Fan: Breakfast of China

Breakfast at the Pig's Inn

To escape the frenetic pace of living in Shanghai, my husband Mark and I would occasionally take the train out to the mountains. In the small village of Xidi, not far from Huangshan (Yellow Mountain), there is a tiny guesthouse of just six rooms owned by the poets Zheng Xiaoguang and Han Yu.

The Pig's Inn is a series of restored private dwellings that at one point in their history were used to house pigs. Today, its guests can be as relaxed as one. You might be familiar with the ancient Hui architecture of the buildings if you have seen the movie *Crouching Tiger, Hidden Dragon*, which was filmed in the nearby village of Hongcun. The interconnected houses have open courtyards and have been decorated in a muted color scheme. They are full of nostalgia for a distant past.

The breakfast served every morning is a feast. The full menu included a green Huangshan vegetable rice (see page 162) with added pickled mustard greens, fried bamboo shoots with mustard greens, rice soup (page 152), steamed bao filled with pork, hard-boiled eggs, eggs scrambled with green peppers, dumplings with vinegar, fried dough sticks, scallion pancakes, and steamed sweet potato for three people.

The menu takes inspiration from the "seven daily necessities" written about in the Song Dynasty book *Dreams of Splendor of the Eastern Capital* by Meng Yuanlao. The book is a retrospective account of Meng's life before the Jin Dynasty conquered the north of China, forcing the Northern Song Dynasty to move to present-day Hangzhou. The seven necessities that Meng describes are firewood, rice, oil, salt, soy sauce, vinegar, and tea. Even 800 years later, they are still relevant for daily life in China, except that perhaps in most homes firewood has been replaced by electricity.

What makes this description of daily life so unique is that Meng's standing in society was very average. He was not a poet, historian, or military commander. He was unpretentious but also deeply emotional about his life. For me, it's representative of the exquisite mundaneness of life that anthropologists have only recently become interested in and which we can often overlook in our lives now. What would we consider the necessities of life to be in the twenty-first century, and would they be at all the same towards of the end of the current millennia? The democratization of photography and social media today is a distant reality from the world of a normal person 800 years ago.

18

Meng describes in gritty detail how his life was before war and exile. Contemporary historians have compared his book to the art of photography, with a focus on composition and an obsession with minute visual detail. He describes the tea houses and inns frequented by different professions, sometimes visiting them street by street to observe the differences. He even watches noodles being made from sheep blood and flour, then served with a sauce that we would recognize today: a mix of ginger, cilantro, and spices. Meng wrote the book from memory, and it is presented as a past dream; a sphere of perfect joy and harmony in which everyday needs were met with ease. Much like the nineteenth century French photographer Cartier Bresson and his understanding of the "decisive moment," Meng describes the fleeting events and moving objects that aligned naturally in his view to be captured.

At the Pig's Inn, it might seem easy to focus on the sheer quantity of the breakfast on the table, but we should also look at the diversity. The whole culinary art of China depends on the art of mixing and balance. Sweet, sour, bitter, and salty, but also savory, or umami, and the less-defined category of *xin* (辛), or "pungency." Volatile ingredients like Sichuan pepper or chile can bring about unpleasant sensations like sweating, watering eyes, or a runny nose, yet in the right dose they impart an irrational addiction, leaving us desperate for more.

The Pig's Inn is a place for us to enjoy the same quiet reflection of a past dream— a simple and fulfilling life, in which history becomes relevant through the daily moments of habit, like the slow consumption of breakfast, before returning to a world of perfect shambles.

20

Mian
Noodles

From fine and slender shapes to bouncy hand-pulled varieties and short, fry-like chunks of starch jelly, Chinese noodles are a symbolic line through time, with over 4,000 years of recorded history behind them and a deep spectrum of meaning, including longevity and prosperity, imbued in them. However you wish to name it, Chinese noodles are the point of origin for the entire category of flour-based doughs cooked in boiling water. Even today, noodles—whether handmade or instant packaged noodles—still sustain millions across continents, from cash-poor students and time-poor professionals to lonely diners enjoying a bowl of ramen.

It's easy for me to simply say "noodles" and for you to understand me, but in Mandarin there is no single word or character that encompasses all noodles. *Mian* (面) can be interpreted as noodles made from wheat flour, while *fen* (粉) can be used to describe noodles made from starch or rice flour. There are also two dominant subcategories, "with soup" (*tang mian*, 汤面) and without (often referred to as "dry," such as Wuhan's hot and dry noodles).

I personally prefer noodles without soup because they offer a greater intensity of flavor. At some noodle shops, especially in Shanghai, to call the liquid served with the noodles a "soup" is a stretch of the definition, as it consists of little more than a few drops of soy sauce and a spoonful of lard in boiling water. Here, the intention is economical: to stretch the volume of the dish in order to fill you up.

For serving sizes of noodles, I find that 3½ oz (100 g) dried noodles will feed two people if you want something that is snackable or part of a larger meal. In Chengdu, it is not uncommon to have two types of noodles and a Guo Kui (see page 94) for breakfast. Further south, where rice noodles are the norm, portion sizes will be sometimes double or even triple this, but rarely eaten with any sort of side dish.

Two key things to remember: never salt your cooking water (we're not in Italy) and always toss and stir vigorously before eating.

Tianshui Mian

甜水面

Sweet Water Noodles
Serves 2

One of the key characteristics of *tianshui mian* (甜水面) is the small portion size, a single portion being only five or six bites. I love that about Chengdu's restaurants: they understand that to make something better is not always to make it larger.

The noodle dough is simple but requires some kneading to achieve its thick and distinctive chew. Unfortunately, this is not a noodle that has a convenient dried substitute, but I make them at home with no machinery and just 12 minutes of active kneading.

You can make the sauce in advance and use it in a multitude of dishes. It goes deliciously with the Xiao Jiaozi on page 217, although for that I like to add a little extra sugar.

This recipe is based on the tianshui mian from the noodle shop opposite the Wenshu Monastery in Chengdu, which the Shangxin Liangfen (see page 65) also come from.

For the sauce
2 tablespoons Fuzhi Jiangyou (see page 278)
1 garlic clove, finely chopped
1 tablespoon Chinese sesame paste
A pinch of granulated sugar
½ teaspoon ground Sichuan pepper
A pinch of MSG
2 tablespoons crushed roasted, unsalted peanuts, or sesame seeds

For the noodles
1⅔ cups (200 g) all-purpose flour
Scant ½ cup (100 ml) water
A pinch of salt

Combine all the sauce ingredients, except for the peanuts or sesame seeds, in a bowl and set aside.

Next, make the noodles. In a large bowl, combine the flour, water, and salt and bring together into a dough with your hands. Knead the dough until it forms a tough-looking ball. It will be difficult to begin with but keep kneading.

Wrap the dough in plastic or cover with a tea towel, then set aside to rest for 15 minutes. Knead again for 3 minutes, then wrap and rest. Repeat this three more times.

Roll out the dough into a ⅛ in (4–5 mm) thick rectangle, then cut it into ⅛ in (4–5 mm) wide strips. Pick up each strip and pull it to increase the length by about 20–30 percent.

Bring a large pot of water to a boil and cook the noodles for exactly 3 minutes.

Divide the noodles between bowls and top with the sauce. Garnish with the peanuts or sesame seeds and then stir, stir, stir!

24

Congyou Banmian

Shanghainese Scallion Oil Noodles

Serves 2

The Shanghainese really love scallions. At Lao Ji Shi, one of my favorite restaurants for dinner, their star dish is the "opium cod head," which is covered in a thick layer of scallions before being steamed. The scallions are removed at the table, leaving their sweet and fragrant aroma behind.

In this dish, scallions are infused slowly in oil to create a pungent dressing that, for me, is an unmistakeable flavor of Shanghai. Just a few tablespoons poured over noodles is transformational. The oil can be made in advance, ready to douse a portion of freshly cooked noodles for a quick breakfast or lunch at home. In fact, this is one of the few dishes I prefer to make at home, as sometimes the sauce served in restaurants

is a little too delicate and I enjoy a rich onion taste. Some restaurants, for example Dong Tai Xiang, do add dried shrimp for an extra dimension of salty umami, but these are definitely optional if you want to keep it vegetarian (or even vegan depending on the noodles you use).

My method differs from the usual wok method, as I prefer to use the oven to slow-roast and confit a large batch of scallions in oil and then finish it with soy and sugar in the bowl. This recipe makes enough for 15–20 portions of noodles. Keep the oil in a jar or airtight container in the fridge, and as long as the scallions are submerged completely in oil it should last for up to a month. You can also use this oil for the Kao Nang on page 130.

Congyou Banmian

1 lb 5 oz (600 g) scallions, cut into 2 in (5 cm) batons
2½ cups (600 ml) neutral oil
3 tablespoons small dried shrimp (optional)
3 tablespoons light soy sauce
2 tablespoons dark soy sauce
2 teaspoons granulated sugar
3½ oz (100 g) dried wheat noodles

Preheat the oven to 350°F (180°C).

Spread out the scallions in an even layer in a roasting pan and pour over the oil, making sure the scallions are covered. Cover the pan with foil and roast in the oven for 90 minutes.

Halfway through, turn the scallions and add the dried shrimp, if using.

When the scallions have shriveled and imparted all their flavor into the oil, remove from the oven and leave to cool.

Pour the oil and scallions into a jar or airtight container, making sure the scallions are completely submerged in the oil.

28

To prepare the dressing, heat 6–8 tablespoons of the scallion oil in a frying pan over medium-high heat (don't add any of the scallions yet), then add the light soy sauce, dark soy sauce, and sugar. Bring to a boil and cook until the sauce has a glossy appearance and the sugar has dissolved. Add 2–3 tablespoons of the confit scallions, then taste and adjust the sweetness or saltiness to your liking.

Bring a large pot of water to a boil and cook the noodles according to the package instructions, then divide the noodles between two bowls and spoon the dressing over the noodles. Garnish with some extra confit scallions, stir vigorously, and serve.

热干面

Re Gan Mian

Wuhan Hot Dry Noodles
Serves 2

Wuhan's hot dry noodles have a cult following among locals. The dish was propelled to national fame during the Covid-19 pandemic, when many of China's youth started making *re gan mian* (热干面) at home and posting their photos on social media in solidarity with the people of Wuhan.

Watching its preparation, you might think this dish is quite simple, but it involves a complex layering of flavors that you don't see in its assembly. The sesame paste differs from its Middle Eastern counterpart because the seeds are first heavily roasted before grinding. The result is a deep brown color and rich nutty flavor without any of the bitterness you might find in tahini. This sesame paste is blended with an infused water called *wei shui* (味水—literally "flavor water") that is made with a variety of spices, with each shop using their own secret recipe. My recipe can be used as a blueprint, but feel free to use any other whole, warming spices you like or to increase the quantity of spices for added intensity of flavor. The finished wei shui can be kept in an airtight container in the fridge for up to 1 month.

This recipe forms one of the trinity of breakfast dishes in Wuhan, along with a side of Mian Wo (page 86) and a plate of delicious San Dou Pi (page 166). It's one of the reasons why many describe the city as the breakfast capital of China.

3–4 tablespoons Chinese sesame paste
2 tablespoons light soy sauce
½ teaspoon Chinese five spice
A pinch of salt
A pinch of granulated sugar
3½ oz (100 g) dried wheat or alkaline noodles
2 tablespoons sesame oil
1 oz (30 g) pickled green beans, diced
1 oz (30 g) cucumber, diced
1¾ oz (50 g) pickled radishes, diced
2 scallions, diced
2 tablespoons whole blanched peanuts, finely chopped
Chile Crisp (see page 282, or use store-bought), to serve

For the wei shui
1 cup (250 ml) water
1 piece of cassia bark or 1 cinnamon stick
1 black cardamom pod
1 star anise
1 bay leaf

Combine all the ingredients for the wei shui in a saucepan and bring to a boil. Boil for 3 minutes, then remove from the heat and set aside to cool.

In a bowl, combine the sesame paste with the soy sauce, five spice, salt, and sugar, then slowly add the wei shui until smooth and pourable.

Bring a large pot of water to a boil and cook the noodles according to the package instructions, then drain and divide between two bowls. Add the sesame oil and toss through.

Divide the fragrant sesame paste between the noodles and top with the pickled green beans, cucumber, radishes, scallions, and peanuts. Finish with the chile crisp, then stir well and enjoy.

31

Shacha Mian

Satay Noodles

Serves 2

It was on a brief jaunt around Fujian province that I really discovered the nuances of *shacha mian*. In the local Hokkien dialect, *shacha* (沙茶) is pronounced "sa te," which hints at the dish's South East Asian origins, where sa te (Romanized as satay) refers to three pieces of barbecued meat on a skewer. Usually served with a peanut sauce, over time satay has become the default name for the sauce itself rather than the skewers.

Shacha mian is often bastardized in the West as any noodle with a large dollop of peanut butter, which is in fact a massive detour from the original concept. The base of the shacha sauce is onion, garlic, chile, dried shrimp, and dried fish in oil, with only a small amount of peanut to finish what is a complex and layered sauce. It is thick and extremely pungent, making it an excellent base for soups and marinades. It is particularly good on eggplants or pork ribs. Make the sauce in advance and when you're feeling a bit peckish, take a spoonful and combine it with your highest-quality nut butter, a splash of coconut or dairy milk, and freshly cooked noodles.

In the city of Xiamen, they top every cup of noodles with a selection of delightfully bouncy, yet uniformly shaped, fish proteins. On the touristy island of Gulangyu, you will find the same noodles, but this time served in aesthetically nostalgic chipped enamel bowls intended to evoke pre-revolutionary China. In Fuzhou, the broth is rich and clingy rather than soupy, and the noodles are topped with the city's signature handmade fish balls.

I prefer to use Cantonese-style egg noodles for this dish, which are sold in supermarkets as "lo mein." The great benefit of this style of noodle is that they can be precooked and then reheated with little loss of texture, which is a technique used in noodle shops when preparing large quantities.

The classic recipe uses only fish balls (and this is what I have included in the recipe overleaf), but meat or other toppings can be added, as seen in the picture opposite.

This recipe makes a large jar of shacha sauce, which is enough for 10–12 bowls of noodles. Keep it in the fridge, covered with a layer of oil, and it will last for up to 1 month. Alternatively, you can portion it into an ice cube tray and freeze it.

Shacha Mian

2 tablespoons smooth peanut butter
6–8 tablespoons coconut milk or whole
    milk (optional)
1⅔–2½ cups (400–600 ml) fish or vegetable stock
4–6 fish balls (optional)
6–7 oz (140–200 g) dried egg noodles

For the shacha sauce
¾ cup (100 g) whole blanched peanuts
1¾ oz (50 g) whole dried chiles
1¾ oz (50 g) dried shrimp
1¾ oz (50 g) small dried anchovies
1¾ oz (50 g) bonito flakes (optional)
1¼ cups (300 ml) neutral oil
1 large onion, finely diced
5–7 garlic cloves, finely chopped
1 teaspoon granulated sugar
1 teaspoon Chinese five spice
Scant ½ cup (100 ml) light soy sauce

To serve (optional)
Cilantro leaves
Roasted, unsalted peanuts, chopped

34

First, make the shacha sauce. In a dry frying pan, toast the peanuts over medium heat for 5–6 minutes until golden brown and fragrant, then remove from the pan and set aside on a plate to cool. Repeat this with the whole chiles, dried shrimp, and dried anchovies, toasting each separately until fragrant and then adding to the plate with the peanuts to cool.

Combine all the toasted ingredients, along with the bonito flakes, if using, in a food processor and blend to a fine sand consistency. Set aside.

Pour the oil into the same pan and gently fry the onion over low heat until soft and lightly golden brown. The aim here is to create a flavored oil, rather than crispy onions. Add the garlic just before the end, then pour in the ground peanut mixture. Add the sugar, five spice, and soy sauce, then cook gently for 10 minutes, stirring often. Keep the heat low and make sure it doesn't burn, otherwise the sauce will be bitter. Remove from the heat and leave to cool completely before transferring to a clean jar.

To prepare the noodles, put 2 tablespoons of the shacha sauce into a saucepan and add the peanut butter, milk, if using, and enough stock to create a soup of your desired thickness. Bring to a simmer and cook until the peanut butter dissolves to create a cohesive sauce.

Meanwhile, bring a large pot of water to a boil and cook the fish balls, if using, according to the package instructions, then remove and set aside. Cook the noodles in the same water according to the package instructions, then drain and divide between two bowls.

Pour over the peanut sauce, then top with the fish balls, a few cilantro leaves, and some crushed peanuts, if using.

Dan Dan Mian

Street Vendor Noodles
Serves 2

The name for this dish comes from the word *dan* (担), meaning a traditional carrying pole that is balanced across the shoulders (see page 11 for a picture of this). One side of the pole would carry noodles and the other would carry the flavorings. In all my time in China, I've never actually seen this dish being sold in this manner, but it's easy to imagine the bustle of a busy Chengdu street in another time.

Today, *dan dan mian* is enjoyed at any time of the day, served in small, snack-sized bowls. Restaurants have their own recipe, but on the table you will find extra chile crisp, vinegar, sugar, and even sometimes MSG so that you can customize your bowl.

Outside of China, for example in Japan, the noodles are often served in a soup. This is called *tantanmen*, the spicy cousin to the similarly Chinese-derived ramen. In Sichuan province, however, they are almost exclusively served dry, with just a simple dressing. Alternatives include a "white oil" (白油) version, without the chile.

1 bok choy, leaves separated
3½ oz (100 g) dried wheat or dan dan noodles
1 tablespoon sesame oil
3½ tablespoons roasted and salted peanuts, chopped
2¼ tablespoons toasted sesame seeds

For the sauce
2 tablespoons Chinese sesame paste
1 teaspoon granulated sugar
2 tablespoons light soy sauce
2 tablespoons chile oil
1 tablespoon lard
2 scallions, chopped
1 teaspoon Sichuan peppercorns, ground
½ teaspoon Chinese five spice
1 teaspoon dried chile flakes or 1 whole dried chile
1 bay leaf
1 garlic clove, finely chopped
1 oz (30 g) fresh root ginger, finely chopped
2⅔ oz (75 g) ground pork
1¾ oz (50 g) zhacai (pickled mustard greens)
1 tablespoon Shaoxing wine
2 tablespoons Sichuan Baoning vinegar

Combine the sesame paste, sugar, soy sauce, and chile oil for the sauce in a bowl and set aside.

Bring a pot of water to a boil and blanch the bok choy for 1 minute until tender. Drain and set aside.

Heat the lard in a frying pan over medium heat and gently fry the scallions, Sichuan pepper, five spice, dried chile, and bay leaf for 1–2 minutes until fragrant. Add the garlic and ginger and fry for a further 2–3 minutes, then add the ground pork with the pickled mustard greens and Shaoxing wine. Cook for a further 3–4 minutes until the meat is golden brown, then remove the bay leaf and whole chile, if using.

Add the chile oil and sesame paste mixture to the pan, then add the vinegar and stir well. Taste and adjust the seasoning as necessary.

Bring a large pot of water to a boil and cook the noodles according to the package instructions, then drain and toss with the sesame oil to prevent them from sticking.

Divide the noodles between two bowls, then dress with the pork sauce and garnish with the chopped peanuts, toasted sesame seeds, and bok choy.

Noodles

Lanzhou Niu Rou Mian

兰州牛肉

Lanzhou Hand-Pulled Noodles in a Spicy Beef Soup
Serves 4

One of the things that is so incredible about Chinese food is the theater of watching it being made to order in open kitchens. The implied message is one of freshness and transparency with the customer. *La mian* (拉面), meaning "pulled noodles," are one of the stars of this show. In steamy kitchens across the country, a ball of soft and pliable dough is formed into a truncheon shape. It is then pressed flat, stretched a little, and then yanked as wide as you can spread your arms.

Very quickly, a single strand goes from one piece to two, then to four, eight, sixteen, thirty-two, and sometimes even sixty-four, turning into delicately thin strands of noodle. Considering the average arm span is about 5 feet (1.5 meters), a bowl of thirty-two strands is an impressive 525 feet (160 meters) of noodles. Observing them close up, you can see subtle and minute variances in the thickness of the noodles, and in the mouth the texture is exciting and springy with a delicious bite. For me, la mian are one of the most delicious noodles in the world. They are usually served suspended in a delicate beef broth, and the chile is deceptively mild despite the intense color.

This dish also has a remarkable history as the progenitor of Japanese ramen after Chinese immigrants settled in Yokohama, Japan, in the late nineteenth century. The hand-pulled noodles changed to knife-cut, but the name persisted.

Another interesting observation is that the locals of Lanzhou don't call this dish la mian, but rather *niu rou mian* (牛肉面), or simply "beef noodle," mostly because of the subtle variations found in the dish across the province of Gansu.

As with all recipes, it's up to you how much effort you want to put into it for the sake of your own piety. In China, many will pay a professional to make the noodles for them or simply buy dried noodles from a supermarket. Using a store-bought, high-quality beef stock or bone broth and infusing it with the aromatics will also save considerable time. If preferred, you can spread this out over three days of preparation by making the soup the day before you make the noodles.

→

39

Lanzhou Niu Rou Mian

For the soup
5½ lb (2.5 kg) beef brisket (or any stewing cut)
2 scallions
1¾ oz (50 g) fresh root ginger, cut into large chunks
4–5 garlic cloves
1 oz (30 g) cilantro leaves
¾ oz (20 g) dried sand ginger or 1¾ oz (50 g) fresh
    galangal (optional)
4–5 whole dried chiles
3–4 bay leaves
2 black cardamom pods
2 star anise
2 cinnamon sticks
1 tablespoon fennel seeds
1 tablespoon Sichuan peppercorns
1 tablespoon long pepper (optional)
1 tablespoon black peppercorns
2 teaspoons ground white pepper
1 tablespoon salt
1 tablespoon rock sugar

For the noodles
4 cups (500 g) all-purpose flour
Generous 1 cup (280 ml) water
1 teaspoon table salt
Neutral oil, for greasing

To serve
A few cilantro leaves
1 scallion, chopped
2–3 teaspoons Chile Crisp (see page 282, or use
    store-bought) or chile oil
Liangban Ziganlan (see page 287)

The day before, make the soup and noodles. Put the beef into a bowl, cover with water, and leave to soak for 1 hour to remove any excess blood or impurities, then discard the water.

Place the beef in a pot and cover completely with fresh water. Bring to a boil, then boil for 3–4 minutes until there is a visible amount of white scum floating on the surface. Reduce the heat to low and use a slotted spoon to remove the scum.

Add all the rest of the ingredients for the soup, then simmer over low heat for 4–6 hours until the beef is tender enough to break apart with the gentle pressure of a fork. Alternatively, transfer to a roasting pan with a lid and cook in the oven at 325°F (160°C) for the same amount of time.

I like to cook the beef this way as you can be sure it won't boil dry. Once cooked, remove the meat from the pot or pan and set aside to cool completely. Remove the spices from the cooking liquid with a slotted spoon and reserve the liquid as the soup base for your noodles. Store the beef and soup in the fridge.

Meanwhile, make the noodles. In a large bowl, combine the flour, water, and salt and bring together into a dough with your hands. Knead for 10 minutes until the dough is smooth and firm, then generously oil the dough and leave it to rest, uncovered, for 30–45 minutes at room temperature to allow the gluten to relax.

Brush a large plate with oil. Using oiled hands, squeeze and shape the dough into a long sausage about as thick as a thumb. Coil the dough on the oiled plate and cover with plastic. Chill in the fridge overnight, or for at least 12 hours.

The next day, remove the dough from the fridge and set aside for about 1 hour to come to room temperature. Break off an 8–12 in (20–30 cm) piece and use your hands to stretch it to double the length. Fold it in half and repeat. If you want very fine noodles, you can do this again.

When you're ready to serve, thinly slice the beef and warm the soup in a pot until gently simmering.

Bring a large pot of water to a boil and cook the noodles in batches for 2 minutes. They won't all float to the surface when cooked, but even if they are a little undercooked it is OK, as they will finish cooking in the bowl.

Ladle some of the hot soup into four bowls, then add the noodles and finish with the cilantro, a pinch of scallions, and the chile crisp or chile oil. Serve with the liangban ziganlan.

41

Qing Tang Mian

Clear Broth Noodles
Serves 2

An enormous cauldron, at least three or four feet across, was bubbling away outside the front door of Man Kou Xiang Zao Can (literally, "a mouthful of fragrant breakfast") in Turpan one morning when my friend Atina and I walked past. "This sort of setup is not cheap," commented Atina.

She is a restaurant owner and my guide in everything to do with Xinjiang. We nodded in agreement that this was going to be a very good breakfast.

It is rare for foreigners to travel so far into these remote areas of Xinjiang, and the owner couldn't contain her excitement. She was a wonderfully smiley woman dressed in bold colors, a bright red headscarf, and a purple jacket who would instinctively pause and pose for the camera.

A ladle with a comically long handle was used to gently prod and stir the cauldron, which was filled with a clear broth dotted with enormous leg bones and a few whole chiles floating on top. While the soup was clearly the focus of the overall dish, the rest of the flavorings brought it to life. A handful of precooked noodles were added to a bowl, then taken outside to the broth. A ladle of soup was poured over to awaken the noodles and then poured back into the pot. Another ladle was poured over the noodles and then

we went back inside. A spoonful of chopped raw garlic was then added, pungent and almost spicy like horseradish or wasabi, followed by a spoon of red chile, finely diced with a little salt to extract some liquid and add a secondary dimension of fresh heat. To garnish, there were a few pieces of finely sliced beef and some raw spinach to add a touch of green. The whole thing was finished with a spoon of Shanxi mature vinegar to add a bright acidity.

The result was a surprisingly pure flavor with each element clearly distinguishable. There was no hiding behind additives or mystery ingredients. It was a dish greater than the sum of its parts.

The morning spread was finished with a selection of *baozi*, cold salads, thin-skinned dumplings dusted with ground cumin (see page 220), and an enormous piece of bone with a sharp knife for cutting off the fat and cartilage.

For this recipe, a high-quality beef bone broth from a butcher or delicatessen will do the job, but if you want to make your own, use the broth recipe on page 262, substituting the pork and chicken for the same weight of beef bones and doubling the simmering time.
→

Qing Tang Mian

3½ oz (100 g) dried or 7 oz (200 g) fresh alkaline
    noodles
3–4 bird's eye chiles
3–4 garlic cloves, chopped or grated into a paste
1 teaspoon water
1¼ cups (300 ml) good-quality beef broth
¼ cup (50 g) spinach, roughly chopped
3–4 thin slices of beef (optional)
2 tablespoons Shanxi mature vinegar
Salt

Bring a large pot of water to a boil and cook the
noodles according to the package instructions,
then drain and rinse under cold water. Set aside.

Reserve one of the chiles and finely chop the rest,
with the seeds. Add the chopped chiles to a bowl
with a small pinch of salt. Stir and set aside.

Put the garlic into a bowl with a small pinch of salt
and the water. Stir and set aside.

Pour the beef broth into a pot and add the
reserved chile, then bring to a gentle simmer.

44 Divide the noodles between two bowls and pour
over the beef broth. Add the spinach and stir it in
until it wilts, then top with a generous spoonful of
the garlic, some chopped chile, and a few beef
slices, if using.

Add a drizzle of vinegar and serve immediately.

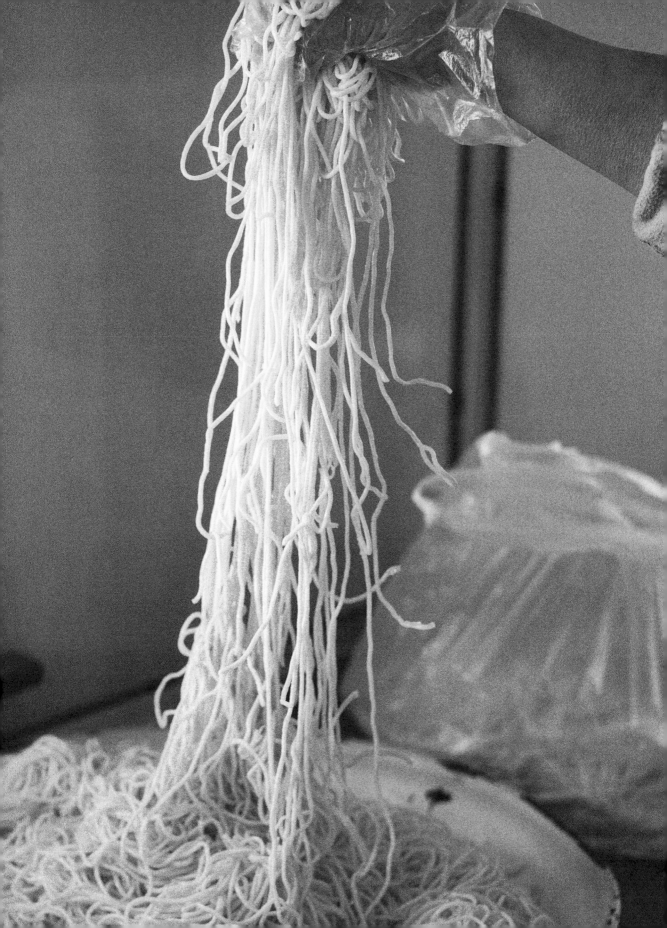

Chongqing Xiao Mian/ Wanza Mian

重庆小面 豌杂面

Chongqing Little Noodles/ Yellow Pea Noodles
Serves 2

Chongqing "little noodles" are small in size but enormous in flavor. The name represents both a specific dish and a category of dishes, and some restaurants sell them as *xiao mian* (重庆小面) while others call them *wanza mian* (豌杂面). No one is quite sure of the difference. Whatever the name, this dish is a fundamental part of Chongqing culinary arts and has played a part in distinguishing it from the cuisine of nearby Chengdu, even though they were once part of the same province.

In the 1990s, China decided to make the city of Chongqing its own city-state, much like Shanghai and Beijing, as the growing metropolis was rapidly expanding beyond the administrative capacity of Sichuan province. Since then, the bureaucratic divide has developed into one of cultural identity between the city and its mother province. Chongqing cuisine has become distinct and, in my opinion, has taken spice to a new level of reckoning, coupled with intense sourness. The palate of the city is bolder and more brash than Chengdu—it's a rock concert rather than a classical symphony.

Making a bowl of these noodles at home is a lot of fun. Pouring smoking-hot oil over spices and aromatics to release the aroma is a dramatic start to the day. And, while all xiao mian start with the same basic principles, you find a lot of diversity in the category: how soupy you want it, if meat is included or not, whether you include additions like potato, and if you go for the all-important garnish of yellow peas or substitute them for chickpeas (or, for those who are supremely lazy, peanuts). If you want to include the meat sauce, it can be made the day before, left to cool, and then stored in the fridge.

The noodles used here are also particular. They are alkaline noodles made with lye water, which gives them a distinctive bite that you may be familiar with from Japanese ramen. It's the same alkaline that gives bagels their characteristic chew. The alkaline prevents the starch from turning mushy in the boiling water and also gives the noodles a yellow tinge, which is why many people confuse them for the egg noodles more commonly found in Cantonese cooking. In restaurants in Chongqing, menus will display prices for bowls of two *liang* (二两) and three liang (三两). A liang (两) is approximately 1¾ oz (50 g), so the portions come with either 3½ oz (100 g) or 5½ oz (150 g) noodles.

→

46

Chongqing Xiao Mian/Wanza Mian

½ cup (100 g) dried yellow peas, whole or split
    (or 1 cup/150 g chickpeas from a can or jar,
    drained)
1½ cups (350 ml) water (if using dried yellow peas)
1 scallion, white and green parts separated,
    both finely chopped
1 garlic clove, finely chopped
1¾ oz (50 g) zhacai (pickled mustard greens),
    half finely chopped
1½ teaspoons chile powder
1 tablespoon roasted, unsalted peanuts,
    chopped, plus a few extra to garnish
½ teaspoon Sichuan peppercorns, ground
1–2 teaspoons white sesame seeds
4–5 tablespoons neutral oil
2 teaspoons light soy sauce
2 teaspoons sesame oil
2 teaspoons Sichuan Baoning vinegar
1 teaspoon lard (optional)
7 oz (200 g) fresh or 3½ oz (100 g) dried alkaline
    noodles
2 leaves of bok choy or romaine lettuce
¼–⅔ cup (60–150 ml) boiling water, broth, or stock
2–3 pieces of boiled potato (optional)

For a simple meat sauce (optional)
2 oz (60 g) ground pork
1 garlic clove, finely chopped
1 thumb-sized piece of fresh root ginger,
    finely chopped
1 shallot or ¼ onion, finely chopped
1 tablespoon Shaoxing wine
1 tablespoon oyster sauce
1 tablespoon light soy sauce
1 tablespoon chile oil

To serve (optional)
Chile Crisp (see page 282, or use store-bought)
Sichuan pepper oil

If you're making the meat sauce, heat a frying pan over medium heat and add the pork. Cook it gently for 5–7 minutes until some of the fat has rendered out, then add the garlic, ginger, and shallot or onion and cook for a further 5–7 minutes. You want the shallot or onion to become slightly translucent and the ginger and garlic to become fragrant, rather than browned.

Add the rest of the ingredients and cook for a further 3–4 minutes so that the flavors can become friends, then remove from the heat and set aside.

Rinse the yellow peas, then transfer to a pot and add the water. Bring to a boil, then reduce to a simmer and cook for 1 hour, uncovered. Check the peas are tender after this time—they may need longer. Drain and set aside. (Skip this step if you're using precooked chickpeas.)

In a heatproof bowl, combine the white part of the scallion, garlic, zhacai, chile powder, peanuts, Sichuan pepper, and sesame seeds.

Heat the oil in a small saucepan over high heat until almost smoking, then very carefully pour it over the aromatics. It will sizzle furiously. Add the soy sauce, sesame oil, vinegar, and lard, then stir well.

Bring a large pot of water to a boil and cook the noodles according to the package instructions. Add the bok choy or lettuce to the water for the last 30–45 seconds. Drain the noodles and divide between two bowls, then add the spicy sauce.

Now you have the option to add extra boiling water to make a simple soup or use a stock or broth of your liking for extra flavor.

Once you've thinned the sauce to your liking, add some of the meat sauce, if using, then the bok choy or lettuce, along with the cooked yellow peas (or chickpeas), potato, if using, scallion greens, chile crisp, and Sichuan pepper oil, if using.

48

Noodles

Mi Xian

Yunnan Rice Noodles

Serves as many as you like

In most instances when I talk about noodle dishes being representative of a place, it's difficult to then also explain how flexible or varied they can be beyond a single recipe. Yunnan province, where these noodles come from, is considerably larger than most European countries, with over 30 unique ethnic minorities and a diverse landscape and ecology that often leads to the area being described as the breadbasket (or should it be rice basket?) of China. It's impossible that a dish like *mi xian* (米线), with its almost infinite varieties, can be explained through one recipe alone. This dilemma is a testament to the enormity of Chinese cooking.

In a breakfast setting or at a restaurant where mi xian is served, there will be a staffed noodle bar where you can select the shape and thickness of your rice noodle. After a few seconds of swirling the fresh noodles in boiling water, the staff member will hand you your bowl and you will take it to the soup and condiment bar. Here you will find a selection of soup bases, including chicken, pork, and vegetable, and up to 30 or even 40 bowls of different soy sauces, herbs, oils, chiles and

chile sauces of various styles, peanuts, tofu pieces, ground pork, nut pastes, pickles, and whatever else the owner likes, the village grows, or the district is famous for.

The influence of this dish has spread into neighboring Guangxi province and over the borders into Thailand and Vietnam. At the vineyard of Miao Lu (see page 70), we even have it for lunch, alongside a large bowl of freshly pressed green Sichuan pepper oil that has the most pleasant numbing quality and a grassy, citrusy, floral spring flavor that is often missing from even the most premium bottled brands.

This is the sort of meal that feeds a crowd. It caters both to those who prefer a light touch and those who want a bowl piled high with every topping and flavor. Get your mise en place looking sharp and the party will look after itself. My advice is to go small on the portions and try everything in one huge medley on your first try, then leave the second round for more individual discernment.

→

Mi Xian

3 oz (80 g) dried or 4 oz (120 g) fresh rice noodles
    per bowl (but you might want seconds or thirds!)
2–3 lettuce leaves per person

For the soup bar
A selection of chicken, pork, beef, or vegetable
    soups/broths of your choice
Or
    1 x quantity Yumi Ersi broth (see page 56)
Or
    1 x quantity Lanzhou Niu Rou Mian soup
    (see page 41)

For the condiment bar
Light and dark soy sauce
Sesame oil
Sichuan pepper oil
Cilantro leaves
Thai basil leaves
Thinly sliced scallions
Toasted white sesame seeds
Roasted peanuts
Chile oil or Chile Crisp (see page 282, or use
    store-bought)
Chinese sesame paste, thinned with some
    hot water
Finely chopped garlic in oil
Pickled radishes
Zhacai (pickled mustard greens)
Lard
Salt
Granulated sugar
MSG or chicken powder

Prepare your mise en place of condiments by
putting everything into small bowls or plates.

If you are using dried rice noodles, cook them
according to the package instructions, then toss
with a few drops of sesame oil to prevent them
from sticking. You can then simply refresh the cold
noodles in boiling water for 45 seconds.

Leave your guests to choose their soup and
condiments, creating their own incredible flavor
combinations!

52

Yumi Ersi

Ersi Noodles with Tomato and Corn Broth
Serves 2

玉米饵丝

This recipe sticks in my memory as I tried it for the first time during one of my research trips for this book. Usually I would have my husband, Mark, or a group of friends at my side when traveling, which is helpful not only for moral support, but also because eating with someone is part of the joy of exploring new areas. This time, however, I was truly on the road on my own. Starting at Miao Lu, the vineyard of my friend Alex (see page 70), I took a car and drove towards the border with Myanmar. While traveling through the serene countryside of Yunnan, I suddenly felt a deep sense of imposter syndrome.

I arrived at Wang Ji Liangfen, a gorgeous courtyard restaurant with balconies overlooking the town of Jianchuan. There was a total sense of calm, with only two or three other customers dining. Immediately, the kindness of the staff put me at ease and

after photographing the dishes with such beautiful presentation and light all my doubts just faded away. I can do this!

The restaurant's most popular dish is not, in fact, the *liangfen* that it takes its name from, but rather its *ersi* (饵丝) noodles, served in a broth flavored with pork, tomato, and corn. The broth is delicate, clear, and full of flavor, made with pork bones and meaty ribs that are cooked with whole corn cobs. Making a clear and intense soup does require some additional steps but I believe it's worth it. Hand-cut ersi noodles are then added to the broth, hidden beneath a layer of toppings that include freshly cut tomato, tofu puffs, spiralized zucchini, hairlike strands of omelet, scallion, pickles, and *la rou* (辣肉), a spicy pork mixture made from the meat from the broth.

→

Yumi Ersi

2 lb 4 oz (1 kg) pork ribs or neck
4¼ cups (1 liter) water
3–4 ripe tomatoes, deseeded
1 corn cob, cut into rounds
4 teaspoons light soy sauce or 4 pinches of salt
1 x quantity Ersi (see page 151)

To serve
1 potato, cut into ⅛ in (3 mm) cubes
1 egg, beaten with 1 tablespoon water
1 scallion, chopped
1 tomato, deseeded and finely diced
2–3 teaspoons zhacai (pickled mustard greens)
2–3 tablespoons finely chopped meat from the
    broth, mixed with Chile Crisp (see page 282,
    or use store-bought)
1 tablespoon crispy pork crackling or scratchings
3½ oz (100 g) zucchini, julienned or spiralized
4–6 tofu puffs
Neutral oil, for frying

Put the pork into a bowl, cover with cold water, and leave to soak overnight. The next day, discard the water. This will remove any excess blood or impurities and help to achieve a clear broth.

Preheat the oven to 325°F (160°C).

Transfer the pork to a large Dutch oven and cover with cold water. Bring to a boil, then cook for 2–3 minutes. Remove from the heat and discard the water. This stage will remove any unwanted smells.

Add the pork back to the pot, cover with water again, and then add the measured water on top of that. Add the tomatoes and corn and bring the pan to a gentle simmer. Most cooks will now tell you to simmer the broth over low heat for 4–6 hours until you have a rich broth, but this is not my preferred method. I prefer to put the lid on the pot and transfer it to the oven to cook for the same amount of time, as this way you get the same result without making your kitchen excessively hot or worrying about the pan boiling dry. If you have an oven with an automatic timer that switches off after a certain time, you could even do this overnight. The purpose of a long and slow cook is to keep the broth clear—the faster the flavor elements in the soup break down, the cloudier broth becomes.

Once cooked, remove the pork and reserve it for the topping. Strain the broth through a fine sieve and discard the corn and tomatoes, then set the broth aside to cool. The broth will keep in the fridge for a week, or for a few months in the freezer.

To prepare the toppings, roast or fry the potato in a little oil until golden brown at the edges.

Heat a little oil in a nonstick pan over high heat and add the egg, tilting the pan to spread it as thinly as possible. Once completely cooked, remove from the pan and allow to cool, then roll it up like a cigar and cut as finely as possible to create hairlike strands of omelet.

When you're ready to serve, warm 2½ cups (600 ml) of the broth in a saucepan. Season with the soy sauce or salt to your liking.

Put the noodles into a large bowl and cover with boiling water. Leave to refresh for 1–2 minutes, then drain and then divide the noodles between two bowls. Add the hot pork broth.

Finish with the toppings. There should be enough to completely conceal the noodles in the bowl beneath. Stir well before serving.

A woman making ersi and erkuai rice cakes in a small factory in Xizhou, Yunnan.

Changfen 肠粉

Steamed Rice Noodle Rolls

Serves 2

Changfen (肠粉, also Romanized as *cheung fun* from Cantonese), can be literally translated as "intestine noodles," which gives us an indication of their appearance. The rippled white skin is not too dissimilar to book tripe or something you'd use to make sausages. Texturally, they are delicate and soft in the mouth, with a gentle sweetness and aroma of rice that is a vehicle for stronger flavors.

One of my most memorable encounters with this dish was in Guangzhou, where I spent a summer teaching workshops for Apple to groups of young Chinese influencers. After a day spent discussing more important matters (i.e. food), they agreed to show me their favorite changfen restaurant for breakfast. The best shops, this spot included, stone-mill their own rice in the restaurant, with a huge machine at the back gently purring as it produces flour as fine as Italian 00 or matcha. The owner of this one proudly told me that he had his own farm, meaning total vertical production.

Finding very finely milled rice flour in the West shouldn't be an issue, as there are brands from Thailand, Japan, and China available almost everywhere. If you can find red or black rice flour, you can even make rather brilliant animal pattern changfen, either by swirling together two batters on a tray or dotting one with another color.

→

Changfen

½ cup (80 g) rice flour
⅔ cup (70 g) rice starch (wheat starch works but
    is less common)
1½ tablespoons cornstarch
1⅔ cups (400 ml) water
Youtiao (see page 77), cut into chunks (optional)
2–3 eggs, beaten (optional)
Chives or scallions, finely chopped (optional)
Neutral oil, for steaming
Chile Crisp (see page 282, or use store-bought)
    or a hot sauce of your choice, to serve

For the dressing
4 tablespoons dark soy sauce
4 tablespoons light soy sauce
4 tablespoons water
2 tablespoons sesame oil
1 garlic clove, finely chopped
A pinch of salt
A pinch of sugar
A pinch of dried shrimp (optional)

Combine the rice flour, rice starch, and cornstarch in a bowl, then gradually add the water, whisking between each addition. It should turn from a smooth paste into a smooth, pourable batter. Set aside.

Next, make the dressing. Combine all the ingredients in a small saucepan and bring to a gentle simmer, then remove from the heat and set aside to cool slightly.

There are a few ways you can go about steaming thin sheets of rice noodle. I own a specially designed machine for this sole purpose that cost me $15 in China, but if you are without one of those, then this is the best alternative.

You will need a wok with a domed lid, a metal steaming rack, a large, flat-bottomed ceramic plate with a lip, and either a spatula or, even better, a dough scraper.

Place the steamer stand in the wok and place the plate on top. Fill the pan with water until it comes halfway up the stand and cover with the lid. Bring the water to a gentle simmer and leave to heat up the plate for about 10 minutes.

Brush the plate with oil, then pour a ladle of the rice batter onto the plate and, using oven gloves or a tea towel, gently tilt the plate to evenly spread out the batter. Cover the pan and steam for 3–4 minutes until set. Give it a poke with a spatula in the corner after this time to see if it has solidified—it may need more time. Use your first attempt to also adjust the quantity of batter—you don't want it to be so thick that it is gummy or too thin that it tears easily.

Using the dough scraper, gently crumple the noodle up and remove it from the plate. Dress the noodle with a few spoons of the sauce and taste for quality control. If you are using *youtiao*, place a couple of chunks at the end of the noodle and carefully roll it up like a jelly roll.

Repeat the process with the rest of the batter, adding a little beaten egg or a scant pinch of chives or scallion if you want to add some flavor and texture.

Once cooked, place the ruffled changfen on a plate and pour over a tablespoon or two of the dressing. Eat immediately with the chile crisp or hot sauce.

If you have any leftover batter, I suggest you cook all of it and store the cooked changfen in the fridge for up to 2–3 days. You can simply steam it back to life.

60

Suanla Fen

Sour Spicy Noodles
Serves 2

Suanla fen are most popular in Chongqing as a breakfast dish or snack eaten throughout the day. *Suan* (酸) means "sour," *la* (辣) means "spicy," and *fen* (粉) is a noodle made with any sort of starch, which in this dish is that of sweet potato. The texture is hilariously slippery and will test the skills of even the most proficient chopstick-user. In the mouth they are chewy and springy, a texture sometimes described as "QQ" which is a little like al dente, but which pushes back against the bite. Dried sweet potato starch noodles are a pantry staple in my home and leftovers can be easily fried.

This dish can be ferociously spicy, served in an eye-watering vinegary soup, or it can dance across the palate with the most luxuriating purr. There is a restaurant in Bologna called BE'MO that serves utterly sensational suanla fen that make me squeal with delight.

The piquant and intense sauce is surprisingly low effort to prepare, making them an ideal breakfast food. A hot bowl of these noodles will open up those sinuses and make your eyes pop open like no cup of coffee ever could!

½ teaspoon chile powder
2 garlic cloves, finely chopped
1 teaspoon toasted white sesame seeds
½ small red chile, sliced
¼–⅓ cup (60–70 ml) neutral oil
4–5 tablespoons rice vinegar or Zhenjiang vinegar
2 tablespoons light soy sauce
½ teaspoon granulated sugar
A large handful of roasted, unsalted peanuts
A pinch of salt
A few sprigs of cilantro
3–3½ oz (80–100 g) dried sweet potato starch noodles (soaked if necessary—check the package)

Put the chile powder, garlic, sesame seeds, and red chile into a heatproof bowl and give it a good stir.

Heat the oil in a small saucepan over high heat until almost smoking, then very carefully pour it over the chile mixture. It will sizzle furiously. Add the rest of the ingredients, except the noodles, and stir well. Season to taste, then divide the sauce between two bowls.

Bring a large pot of water to a boil and cook the noodles according to the package instructions, then drain, reserving some of the cooking water.

Divide the noodles between the bowls and add some of the cooking water to create a soup to your preference—personally, I don't like it too soupy. Serve immediately.

Liangfen

Starch Jelly Noodles
Serves 4 generously

Starch is a wonderful ingredient in any kitchen. Commonly used to thicken sauces in both Western and Asian kitchens, you also find it in the form of chewy noodles or jiggly jellies across China, Korea, and South East Asia. These constitute an entire subcategory of noodles, which are often served cold alongside incredibly spicy sauces.

Almost any starch is suitable for making starch jelly, but the most common in China are those derived from sweet potatoes, yellow peas, or mung beans. Sweet potato is my personal favorite because it is less soluble in water, giving a firmer and less mushy texture. The downside of sweet potato starch is that it's terrible for thickening sauces because of its intense strength. Conversely, if you use cornstarch, you'll end up with a starch that is too soft to cut and manipulate.

For soft jelly noodles, I think mung bean and yellow pea are the best choice, as they both offer the same satisfying soft-set jiggle and are widely available. Making a batch yourself not only gives you noodles, but you can cut the jelly into cubes and fry it for an extra sensory experience.

Just remember that to make your jelly firmer, it is not a question of simply adding more starch. You need a stronger starch, not more of the same. You can try experimenting with blending different starches, but a good place to start is a ratio of one part starch to eight or nine parts water.

Once you've made your starch jelly noodles, toss them with your own blend of sauce or use them in the recipes on pages 65 and 67.

5¾ cups (1.35 liters) water
5½ oz (150 g) mung bean, yellow pea, or sweet potato starch

Combine 1 cup (240 ml) of the water with the starch in a bowl and set aside.

Pour the rest of the water into a pot and bring to a boil. Once boiling, turn the heat down low and whisk in the starch paste. Gently heat the mixture, stirring continuously, until it starts to transform into a semi-transparent and thick gel-like consistency.

Pour the thickened starch mixture into a bowl and leave to cool for at least 1 hour before chilling in the fridge overnight until it has solidified.

The next day, turn the starch jelly out onto a board and cut it into your desired shape—the most common are long, thin noodles, fat fry-length batons, or chunky cubes.

Shangxin Liangfen

伤心凉粉

Heartbreak Noodles

Serves 2

There are two theories as to why these are called "heartbreak" or "sadness" noodles. One is that their intense spiciness will break your heart and bring tears to your eyes. The other is that if you are heartbroken, eating these noodles will distract your senses enough to forget about it, just for a moment. Either way, intensity of flavor is key here. Make sure your starch jelly is fridge-cold when you cut it, to offset the heat of the sauce. The contrast of cold noodle and spicy sauce makes a very pleasant summer breakfast or snack.

While the common translation for the *liangfen* in this dish is "noodles" (that generic term for everything), traditionally, this recipe features batons of cold starch jelly that are stacked—rather testing, even for proficient chopstick users.

This recipe is inspired by the *shangxin liangfen* sold at a small shop opposite the Wenshu Monastery in Chengdu (shown bottom). Served in small portions, it uses both chile crisp and fresh chile, along with plenty of fresh, fiery garlic.

3–3½ oz (80–100 g) Liangfen (see page 63), cut into batons
1–2 red chiles, deseeded and finely chopped
3½ tablespoons roasted, unsalted peanuts, chopped
2 garlic cloves, finely chopped
1 small piece of fresh root ginger, about the same size as the garlic, finely chopped
3 tablespoons Fuzhi Jiangyou (see page 278)
2 tablespoons Zhenjiang vinegar
1 teaspoon sesame oil
½ teaspoon granulated sugar
A pinch of MSG
1 scallion or 3–4 chives, chopped

Divide the starch batons between two bowls. Top with the fresh chile and peanuts.

Put the garlic and ginger into a separate small bowl and add the remaining ingredients, then stir to combine.

Pour the sauce over the noodles, then garnish with the scallion or chives and serve.

65

Huasheng Liangfen

花生凉粉

Peanut Sauce Jelly Noodles

Serves 1

When dining at Wang Ji Liangfen in the small town of Jianchuan, Yunnan (see page 54), I was surprised to see a peanut-based sauce for *liangfen*. Sesame paste is the favored nutty flavoring across most of China and peanuts are usually reserved for garnishing. Then it dawned on me that Jianchuan is only 70 miles (110 km) from the border with Myanmar and virtually all Burmese cooking uses peanuts. (The border between the two countries is over 1,250 miles/2,000 km long and it is largely porous.)

3–3½ oz (80–100 g) Liangfen (see page 63)
1 tablespoon Fuzhi Jiangyou (see page 278)
1 teaspoon Zhenjiang vinegar
1 tablespoon Lijiang Chile Paste (see page 279)
1 tablespoon chunky peanut butter, loosened with
    4–5 tablespoons water
A handful of cilantro, chopped
½ scallion, chopped

Put the noodles into a bowl, then add the sauces in layers—first the infused soy sauce and vinegar, then the chile paste, and finally the peanut butter. Add the cilantro and scallion to make it pretty, then stir and enjoy.

Mian Bao
Breads and Doughs

The spectrum of bready, doughy breakfast items in China is enormous. From steamed Bao (see page 115) made with wheat flour and fried Mian Wo (see page 86) made with fermented rice to naturally fermented sourdoughs and commercially yeasted offerings, every province has some sort of bread at breakfast.

One of the unique features of the recipes in this chapter is their portability. Generally speaking, they're eaten by hand and often while standing. Whereas noodles require boiling water to cook the dough, a bowl to eat from, tools and utensils, and most importantly a seat, bread breaks free from those conditions. There are so many times that I have been sustained on a long trip by buns hastily tossed into a plastic bag, and countless instances that I have stopped in a convenience shop for a late-morning snack chosen from a steamy glass box, all for as little as 2RMB (about a quarter).

These dishes are not always a complete meal in themselves—sometimes they're torn and dunked into something, used to mop up the sauce from a bowl of noodles, or added as a filling or topping for texture. The varied cooking methods applied to these doughs, like baking, frying, and steaming, provide textures that range from flaky and crunchy to soft and pillowy.

The character *mian* (面) here describes the base ingredient, wheat flour, and the second character, *bao* (包), literally means "bag," or in this case an enclosed dough filled with delicious flavors. It might seem an easy job to categorize foods to go into this chapter, but it is not. There is great variety to be found. But instead of singling out the oddities, I would prefer to make a virtue of them. The Wuhan favorite *mian wo*, for example, is rice-based. Shanghainese *sheng jian bao* (生煎包) have many varieties, some with thin skins that place them closer to something in the dumpling category. Likewise, a *xiao long bao* (小笼包), despite being very much a bao by name, feels more at home in the dumpling category. Here I am simply using my intuition.

Baba

Breakfast Bread at Miao Lu
Makes 2–3 breads

粑
粑

At 1.7 miles (2.75 km) above sea level, Miao Lu in Yunnan is one of the highest vineyards in the world. With the Jade Dragon Snow Mountain as a backdrop, the altitude literally takes your breath away. The owner, Alex Xu (one of my dearest friends), describes it as a place of pure pleasure. I have learned much from his passion and long-term vision for viticulture in China.

The first time I visited, we arrived in total darkness in the early hours of the morning after our flight from Shanghai to Lijiang was horribly delayed. The team had prepared us an absolute feast that we devoured late in the night. A fresh tofu dish was on the table that survives only in my memories. A few hours later, we woke to a breakfast that I could eat every day until the end of time.

At the center of everything was the *baba* (粑粑), a simple round bread typical of the province. Keep in mind that Yunnan is considerably larger than most European countries, so this bread is made in a multitude of styles, sizes, and flavors. At Miao Lu, a decade-old sourdough starter is central to the quality of the experience.

A ball of the baba dough is rolled into a circle and is delicately fried on both sides. It puffs up immediately, reminiscent of Indian *bhatura* or Italian *gnocco fritto*. On the table, it is orbited by other dishes, including *furu* (腐乳), a fermented tofu that in Yunnan is packed in chile and which evokes notes of pungent cheese. It is spreadable, creamy, and alluring—I don't know anyone who hasn't been entranced by its magical aroma. The table is completed with frilly edged fried eggs plated with a judicious drizzle of soy sauce, fried slices of Chinese ham that resemble Canadian bacon and small rounds of steamed corn.

Everyone has their own approach. I like to take a wedge of baba and split it open, smear it with furu, and then top it with a slice of fried ham and an egg with a slightly oozy yolk. It is pure bliss, heightened by the dizzy headiness of being so high in the mountains. Between bites you need to take a couple of deep, restorative breaths.

As with all dough recipes, it can be difficult to provide exact instructions, as experience and intuition are key to understanding if the dough is relaxed enough or needs more kneading. Similarly, all sourdough starters react differently and the autolyse stage and bulk rise stages will vary enormously. In the interest of having a breakfast with minimal fuss, prepare your dough the night before and leave it to proof in the fridge overnight, allowing it to come to room temperature before frying. This recipe can only really be replicated if you have a decent sourdough starter at home. If you don't, I urge you to get one going and source a jar of Yunnan-style chile furu.

→

Baba

7 oz (200 g) sourdough starter
2½ cups (300 g) all-purpose flour
⅔ cups (150 ml) lukewarm water
1 teaspoon salt
Neutral oil, for greasing and frying

To serve
Yunnan-style fermented tofu
Fried back bacon or Chinese ham if you can find
    it (not too crispy; optional)
Fried eggs, drizzled with soy sauce or Fuzhi
    Jiangyou (see page 278)
Steamed corn on the cob, cut into rounds
1 bottle of good-quality white Burgundy or
    Champagne

Combine the sourdough starter, flour, water,
and salt in a bowl and use your hands to bring it
together into a rough dough. Cover and leave to
rise at room temperature for 30–45 minutes, or
until doubled in size.

With wet hands, stretch the dough and fold one
side over the other. Cover again and transfer to
the fridge to rest overnight.

The next day, remove the dough from the fridge
30–60 minutes before you want to cook. You
should have a soft, pliable dough that is not too
dissimilar to pizza dough.

Oil a work surface, then weigh the dough and
divide it into two or three equal-sized pieces.
Shape the dough to the size of your frying pan.

Pour a generous amount of oil into the pan and
place it over high heat. Bring it almost to smoking
point, then turn the heat down a little and gently
fry one of the breads for 30–45 seconds on each
side. You want it to be cooked through but barely
golden brown. Drain on paper towels, then cut into
quarters.

Repeat with the remaining dough, then serve
breads with the sides.

In the tradition of Miao Lu, once you have finished,
celebrate the start of the day by opening a bottle
of wine, preferably good white Burgundy or
Champagne.

72

Youtiao

油条

Fried Dough Sticks

Makes 6–8 sticks

Youtiao are a cornerstone of Chinese breakfasts. *You* (油) means "oil" and *tiao* (条) is a stick or something long. They can be eaten alone, but are usually dipped into soy milk or rice porridge or used as part of other dishes such as Jianbing Guozi (see page 78) and Ci Fan Tuan (see page 158). They are also common in many styles of hotpots, Cantonese dim sum and, more recently, they have found fame as a dessert, topped with soft serve ice cream or split open and stuffed with sticky rice mochi. These fried dough sticks are eaten in every region of China as well as wherever you find Chinese communities overseas. Variations are found in Hong Kong, Malaysia, Singapore, Thailand, and in Chinatowns around the world.

The dough for youtiao uses both yeast and baking powder as leavening agents and it is left to ferment for 24 hours. This creates an incredibly light interior that is fluffy and airy and a crisp, delicate exterior. One of the most common deviations from the standard recipe is the addition of milk powder to the dough, but I have tried them side by side in the breakfast market in Qingdao and can confirm the difference is negligible. Even though they are fried, a good youtiao should never be greasy.

The method of shaping them is unique, too. The dough is rolled out and cut into 4–5 in (10–12 cm) fingers, then one is placed on top of the other and they are pressed down in the middle with a chopstick. The piece is then stretched by hand to a length of 16–20 in (40–50 cm) and finally dropped into hot oil where it is quickly fried.

If you don't have a pan big enough to make full-sized youtiao, many home cooks will make short, nugget-sized versions in a regular pan or wok. Leftovers can be cut into slices and fried a second time to make a frugal topping for virtually anything, from soups to sandwiches and salads.

75

Breads and Doughs

Youtiao

2 cups (250 g) strong white bread flour, plus extra
    for dusting
1 cup (240 ml) warm water
¼ oz (7 g) envelope instant yeast
2 teaspoons granulated sugar
½ teaspoon baking powder
1 teaspoon salt
1 tablespoon neutral oil, plus extra for frying

The night before you want to eat, combine all
the ingredients in a large bowl or a stand mixer
fitted with the dough hook attachment. Knead
by hand for 12–15 minutes or in the stand mixer
for 6–8 minutes until you have a smooth and
soft dough. Cover and leave to rise at room
temperature for 45–60 minutes, or until doubled
in size.

Once risen, knock the dough back and return to
the bowl. Cover again. If it is summer, transfer the
dough to the fridge to rest overnight. Otherwise,
leave in a cool place.

The next morning, remove the dough from the
fridge and bring it to room temperature. Roll the
dough on a lightly floured surface into a long
rectangle, around 4–5 in (10–12 cm) wide and
12–14 in (30–35 cm) long.

Cut the dough into fingers about 1–1½ in (3–4 cm)
wide and 4–5 in (10–12 cm) long.

Meanwhile, heat 1–1½ in (3–4 cm) oil in a large
pot, deep frying pan or wok until it reaches 350°F
(180°C).

Take one piece of dough and place it on top of
another. Place a chopstick or skewer on top
lengthways and press hard enough to fuse the
two dough fingers together.

Gently stretch the youtiao at either end to make
it longer—you want it to be about 3–4 times the
original length. If your pan is too small, you can
cut them in half or thirds so they fit.

Fry each youtiao for 3–4 minutes on each side
until golden brown, then remove and drain on
paper towels.

Jianbing Guozi

Northern Chinese Folded Crêpe
Makes 3–4 crêpes

煎饼果子

Whenever I have been away from Shanghai for any extended period of time, one of the first things I eat on my return is a *jianbing* (煎饼). Particularly, one from my jianbing lady on the corner of Xiangyang and Yongkang Lu. I featured her in another book I wrote, *Eat Like a Local SHANGHAI*, and I use her as the benchmark to judge and rank all others. I love jianbing so much that in 2020 I was even a judge for a jianbing competition in Shanghai.

Arguably one of China's most loved breakfast items, the average price for a jianbing is around 6–7RMB (about $1). It consists of a thinly made pancake that is topped with egg, a thin cracker called a *baocui* (薄脆), a sweet sauce made from fermented wheat called *tianmianjiang* (甜面酱), scallion, cilantro, and a little chile crisp. There are customizable options, too: shredded potato, bacon, Chinese sausage, *youtiao*, or extra egg.

The whole thing is made at lightning speed and consumed almost as quickly. Having your mise en place prepared is crucial for making jianbing as the construction of the pancake takes less time than actually eating it. You don't want to be fussing over ingredients, because when the time comes you need to have everything chopped and ready and in the correct order so that the jianbing comes together in perfect harmony.

Originally from Shandong province, jianbing is sometimes also called *jianbing guozi* (煎饼果子). This is because *guozi* is the name for youtiao in the local dialect of Tianjin, and youtiao sometimes takes the place of the crispy baocui.

The batter is made from a mixture of grains. It is mostly wheat flour, but can also include mung bean or millet flour or a mixture of starches, and each vendor will have their own secret recipe. The griddle used to cook jianbing is the same piece of equipment that is used to make French crêpes, but it can easily be done in a frying pan at home with just a little practice.

→

Jianbing Guozi

2½ cups (300 g) all-purpose flour
3 tablespoons wholewheat flour
2 tablespoons soy bean flour or cornstarch
2 tablespoons mung bean flour
1 teaspoon baking powder
1 tablespoon neutral oil, plus extra for frying
1½ cups (365 ml) water

**For the cracker (or use 2 store-bought
dumpling wrappers per jianbing)**
¼ cup (30 g) all-purpose flour
1 tablespoon water
Neutral oil, for frying

For the filling
3–4 eggs
3 scallions, chopped
¾ oz (20 g) pickled radishes, finely diced
A handful of cilantro, chopped
2–3 tablespoons tianmianjiang
3–4 Youtiao (see page 77)
Chile Crisp (see page 282, or use store-bought),
    chile oil, or another hot sauce, to taste

80

Prepare the batter by whisking together all the ingredients in a bowl. Set aside to rest while you make the crackers.

Combine the flour and water in a small bowl. At first it will seem very dry but keep working it for 5 minutes and it will come together into a smooth and tight dough.

Roll out the dough into a long oval and fold it into thirds, then roll it out again. Repeat this five times.

Divide the dough into three equal pieces and roll each piece into a thin square, about 6 x 6 in (15 x 15 cm). Make a short cut in the middle about 2 in (5 cm) long (this will keep the cracker flat when frying). Heat ½–¾ in (1–2 cm) oil in a small frying pan over medium-high heat. Fry the crackers for a few seconds on each side until golden brown, but be careful as they can burn very easily. Drain on paper towels.

Grease a jianbing griddle or frying pan and place over high heat. Once hot, quickly pour a ladleful of batter onto the pan and spread it around the pan evenly. Scrape off any excess batter into a bowl. It's better to have excess rather than not enough to cover the surface.

By the time you finish pushing the batter around the pan, it should be almost cooked.

Immediately crack an egg onto the pancake and use a spatula to spread it out, breaking the yolk.

Scatter over some of the scallions, pickled radishes, and cilantro.

Fold the edge nearest to you towards the middle, then spread on the sauce and add a cracker and a youtiao. Fold in the other side to create two straight edges, then roll up the jianbing completely and cut in half. Serve immediately.

Congyou Bing

Scallion Pancakes

Makes 6 pancakes

Scallion pancakes can be thin and flaky with layers that easily pull apart or thicker and stout, more like a crunchy puck of dough. One of the most iconic producers was A Da in Shanghai, where the proprietor opened at 5 a.m. to an almost immediate line of die-hard customers. I went, once, hours before sunrise, as the shop was not far from my house.

The owner had a large hunchback from leaning over an enormous metal pan, pressing fat bundles of dough into oil for decades. Customers were allowed a maximum of five pancakes each and he only took cash. Unfortunately, he had no successor, so the signature style of A Da is now a closed chapter in the breakfast story of Shanghai.

Nowadays, the flaky variety of *shou zhua bing* (手抓饼) from Taiwan has become more mainstream, not simply because it tastes good, but also because it looks good on social media. Many recipes use a combination of oil and flour to create layers, but I find that this can taste like raw flour and has an unpleasant sandy texture.

Unfortunately, if you are vegetarian or vegan it is genuinely your only option, otherwise the best fat to use is lard.

5 cups (600 g) all-purpose flour, plus extra
  for dusting
1¼ cups (300 ml) water
3½ tablespoons neutral oil
1 teaspoon salt
½ cup (100 g) lard, softened (or 3½ tablespoons
  neutral oil mixed with 2 tablespoons
  all-purpose flour)
12 scallions, finely chopped
Ground white pepper, to taste

Combine the flour, water, oil, and salt in a bowl, then use your hands to bring it together into a smooth dough. Knead the dough for 10 minutes, then cover and leave to rest at room temperature for 30 minutes.

Roll out the dough on a lightly floured surface into a large rectangle around 14 x 28 in (35 x 70 cm).

Smear the lard (or the oil and flour paste) across the entire surface of the dough, sprinkle the scallions over one side in an even layer, and press them into the dough. Sprinkle as much white pepper as you like across the dough—I like a hefty amount.

Fold the rectangle in half to make a square and press down on it, as if you were making a big square sandwich. Cut the dough into thin strips, about ½ in (1 cm) wide. Give them all a stretch so they double in length.

Divide the strips into six bundles, then, like making fresh tagliatelle, coil each bundle around your fingers into a snail. Flatten the snail into a pancake and repeat with the remaining dough. Cover with a tea towel and set aside to rest for 15 minutes.

Meanwhile, preheat the oven to 300°F (150°C).

Heat a dry frying pan over medium heat. Roll out one of the pancakes to at least 8 in (20 cm) wide, then fry for 4–5 minutes on each side until golden brown. If you want, you can brush with a little neutral oil or any leftover lard you have, but the amount of fat in the dough should be enough by itself. Repeat with the remaining pancakes, then transfer to a baking sheet and cook in the oven for 10–15 minutes until cooked all the way through.

葱油饼

Baursak

Бауырсақ
Fried Kazakh Breads
Makes 25–30 pieces

In the city of Yining, on China's far western border with Kazakhstan, all the houses of the old town are painted a vivid blue. The reason is rather lovely: as a city extremely far from any ocean, the color reminds the residents of the world beyond their view. It's the sort of optimism required to live in an area that has been subject to power struggles between empires and warlords for centuries.

On one of the mornings I was there, I found myself in a restaurant called Baursak, named after their most famous dish, a fried nugget of dough that puffs up like a balloon. Common in many Central Asian cultures, they are served for breakfast with fresh jams that remind me of the type Russians use to sweeten their tea, salty, canary-yellow butter and a portion of chilled sour cream that has a wonderful acidic tang.

The breads could be confused for Italian *gnocco fritto* or Mexican *chimangos*, and are a thrifty way to use up leftover dough. In the Kazakh community, they make them throughout the day and use them in both sweet and savory dishes to mop up sauces, much like the way Han Chinese would use white rice.

They are also served with the salty milk tea that the Xibonese people prepare (see page 178) but at Baursak, the tea is finished with crispy millet and puffed rice for extra texture and crunch.

One stylistic difference: the Kazakh community in China cut their *baursak* into squares, while across the border in Kazakhstan, circles are more common.

2 cups (250 g) strong white bread flour, plus extra for dusting
¼ oz (7 g) envelope instant yeast
⅓ cup (70 ml) water
⅓ cup (70 ml) whole milk, at room temperature
1 egg, at room temperature
1 tablespoon unsalted butter, softened, or 2 tablespoons neutral oil
A pinch of salt
Neutral oil, for frying

To serve
Jam or fruit compote
Salted butter
Soured cream
Nai Cha (see page 178)

Put all the ingredients, except the oil for frying, into a stand mixer fitted with the dough hook attachment and mix for 8–10 minutes until you have a smooth and soft dough.

Tip out the dough, then bring it together with your hands into a smooth ball. Transfer to a clean bowl, cover, and leave to rise at room temperature for 45–60 minutes, or until doubled in size.

Roll out the dough on a lightly floured surface to ⅛ in (5 mm) thick, then cut it into 2 x 2 in (5 x 5 cm) squares. In Yining the chef used a wavy ravioli cutter, but a knife will do the same job.

Heat 2 in (5 cm) oil in a large saucepan, deep frying pan, or wok until it reaches 325°F (160°C). The goal here is to create steam inside the dough that will escape, creating a hollow interior. If the temperature is too high, the exterior will cook before it has a chance to expand.

Fry the pieces of dough in batches for 2–3 minutes on each side, flipping them once they start to puff up. Once cooked, remove and drain on a wire rack or paper towels.

Serve warm with the jam, butter, sour cream, and *nai cha*.

Mian Wo

面窝

Savory Rice-Flour Fritters
Makes 8–10 fritters

With a thick, doughnut-like edge and crisp, shattering center, *mian wo* (面窝) are an indispensable part of the morning routine in Wuhan. Perfectly matched with a bowl of Re Gan Mian (see page 31), just break them into small pieces and dip them into the sauce once the noodles have been eaten.

Despite the use of the character mian (面), they are not made from wheat flour, but rather rice.

Keeping with the tradition of street-food vendors finding innovative uses for hardware tools, you can customize a regular ladle to make these by turning it over and hammering a bump into the bowl. This will create the thinner middle that is characteristic of mian wo.

¼ cup (50 g) dried soy beans
2½ cups (500 g) long-grain rice
1 teaspoon salt
1¾ oz (50 g) scallions or chives, finely chopped
1 tablespoon very finely chopped fresh root ginger
2 teaspoons sesame oil
Neutral oil, for frying

Put the soy beans into a bowl and cover with water, then leave to soak overnight.

Wash the rice, then cover with water and leave to soak for 2 hours.

Drain the water from both and transfer the rice and soy beans to a blender. Blend to a smooth paste, then add enough water to make a pourable batter. Add the salt, scallions or chives, ginger, and sesame oil.

Meanwhile, heat 3–4 in (7–10 cm) oil in a large pot, deep frying pan, or wok until it reaches 350°F (180°C). The oil needs to be at least as deep as your ladle is wide.

Place the customized ladle in the oil to heat it up. Using a second, regular ladle, pour enough batter into the customized ladle so that the bump is just covered and submerge it into the oil gently. After a few seconds a crust will form and the mian wo will self-release. After 20 seconds, flip it and cook on the other side. Once golden brown all over, remove and place on a wire rack or paper towels to drain. Repeat with the remaining batter.

Any leftover batter can also be frozen.

86

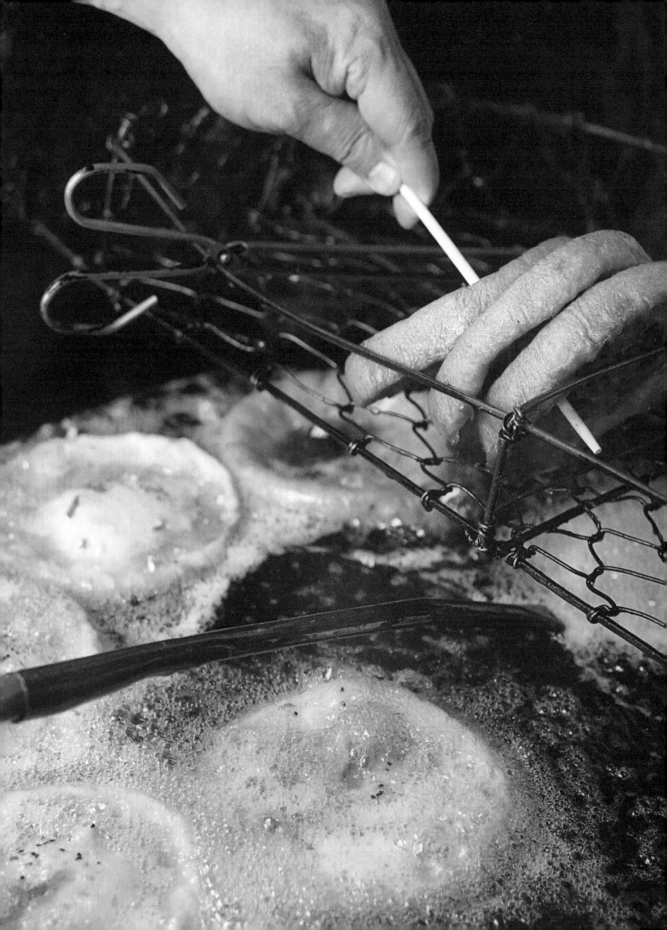

Jiao Quan

Fried Dough Rings
Makes 10–12 rings

These crunchy, golden bracelets of dough are a familiar sight in Beijing cafés and at street-side breakfast vendors. A long time ago they were called *xiao you gui* (小油鬼), or "little oil ghosts," and some suburban restaurants in the capital still use this phrase, although it's almost extinct in the central areas.

Every region of China has its own version of a crispy piece of dough that contrasts with something soupy or porridge-like and most cities have groupings of dishes, almost always a trio, that are considered perfect bedfellows, although they're not always breakfast items.

Serve these alongside a bowl of hot soy milk or the Miancha from page 146 and some thinly sliced pickles for a holy trinity of Beijing breakfasts.

2 cups (250 g) all-purpose flour, plus
    extra for dusting
½ teaspoon baking powder
½ teaspoon baking soda
A pinch of salt
⅔ cups (150 ml) warm water
2 tablespoons neutral oil, plus extra for frying

Combine all the ingredients in a large bowl, then use your hands to bring it together into a smooth dough. The dough should leave the sides of the bowl clean and be firm to the touch.

Knead the dough for 10 minutes, then cover and leave to rest at room temperature for 15 minutes. Repeat this process twice more. This can be done the night before and the dough chilled in the fridge overnight, but make sure it comes to room temperature before shaping.

Roll out the dough on a lightly floured surface to around 2 mm thick, then cut it into strips about ¾ in (2 cm) wide and 4–5 in (10–12 cm) long. Take a strip and fold it in half widthwise, then cut a long incision along the length of the strip of dough, leaving the ends intact, and pull it open like a mouth. This is your dough ring ready to fry. Repeat with the remaining dough strips.

Meanwhile, heat 1–1½ in (3–4 cm) oil in a large pot, deep frying pan, or wok until it reaches 350°F (180°C).

Fry the *jiao quan* in batches of 2 or 3 for 3–5 minutes until golden brown and crunchy. You are looking for a blistered texture on the surface of the dough. Drain on a wire rack or paper towels.

Su De Diao Zha Zha Rou Bing

酥得掉渣炸肉饼

Meat Pies Stuffed with Fish Mint
Makes 6 pies

A few years ago, I visited Anshun in Guizhou with my friend, Henrietta. We were there for a tea expedition that started in Guizhou and worked its way south into Yunnan. Of all the curious foods of the province, the two stand-out breakfast items were the *douhua* (豆花), a kind of tofu pudding with copious amounts of toppings (see page 197), and the meat pies, not too dissimilar from the Guo Kui (see page 94) of Chengdu or many other meat-filled parcels across China. The method for making the crispy pastry exterior is different to *guo kui* or a European laminated pastry such as a croissant, however. At Time-Honored Xinqiao Luoji Meat Pie Shop, which we visited, the dough is rolled out, cut into long strips like noodles, and then bundled up into a ball. The dough ball is then flattened gently by hand, stuffed with plainly flavored pork, and then sealed like any other *baozi* would be, by pinching in a circular motion until closed. But it doesn't end there.

The buns are deep-fried until gloriously flaky, and then, before eating, they're split open and stuffed with a hefty fistful of *zhe er gen* (折耳根), a spindly looking white root that is roughly chopped and mixed with chile and vinegar. This plant (*Houttuynia cordata*) has a rather surprisingly astringent fish flavor, giving us the common English name, fish mint (also known as chameleon plant). It's easier than you might think to find it in Asian supermarkets because of its popularity in Vietnamese cooking. The people of Guizhou almost exclusively eat the roots raw and cold.

I like to julienne the fish mint to create a slaw-like texture. Dressed with a touch of vinegar it cuts through the fattiness of the pies. It's also used as a topping for crinkle-cut fries at street stalls in Chengdu, which are absolutely worth seeking out. If you can't get hold of fish mint, you could substitute daikon, regular mint, and fish sauce to try to replicate the texture and flavor. It won't be quite the same, but it will still be delicious.

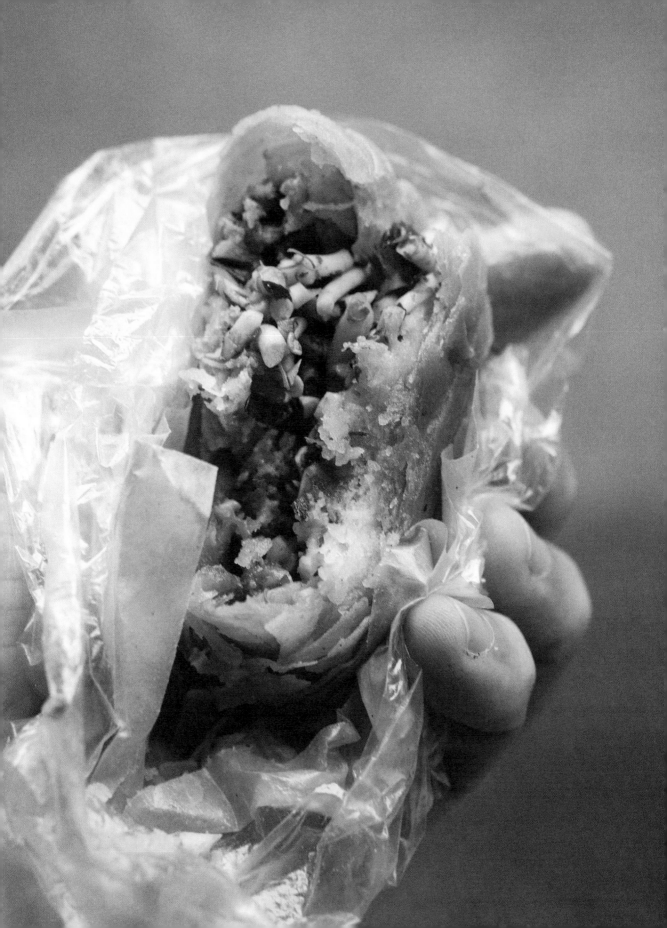

Su De Diao Zha Zha Rou Bing

For the fish mint stuffing
3½ oz (100 g) fish mint roots
2 tablespoons chile oil
3½ tablespoons rice vinegar
2 scallions, finely chopped

For the dough
2½ cups (300 g) all-purpose flour
¾ cup (170 ml) water
1 teaspoon instant yeast
2 teaspoons lard
1 teaspoon salt
1 teaspoon ground white pepper
Neutral oil, for frying

For the filling
7 oz (200 g) fatty ground pork (around 15% fat)
¾ oz (20 g) fresh root ginger, finely chopped
1–2 teaspoons ground Sichuan pepper,
   depending on your taste
3 tablespoons cold water
A pinch of salt

First, prepare the fish mint stuffing. Clean the roots of any brownish hairs and trim them. You want white, matchstick-lengths of root. I like to cut them on the diagonal so they have more surface area to soak up the marinade. Put the prepared roots into a bowl with the chile oil, vinegar, and scallions and stir. Set aside to marinate.

Combine all the ingredients for the dough, except the oil, in a bowl and use your hands to bring the mixture together into a firm ball. It should come away cleanly from the sides of the bowl. Knead the dough for 8–10 minutes until smooth and springy, then cover and leave to rest at room temperature for 1 hour.

Meanwhile, prepare the filling. Combine all the ingredients in a bowl, then use your hand in a claw shape to mix the meat in one direction and one direction only. This will help whip the protein structure, creating a light and delicate texture.

Weigh the dough and divide it into six equal pieces, then roll one piece into a strip about 2–2½ in (5–6 cm) wide and 25–12 in (30 cm) long. Using a knife or a pasta cutter, cut long strips about ¼ in (6 mm) thick (it should look like tagliatelle pasta).

Roll the strips up into a ball from one end, then repeat until you have six bundles of dough strips. Take one ball and flatten it gently in your hands into a roughly 4 in (10 cm) circle. Add a generous amount of the filling and then wrap the dough over the filling and seal it up. When sealing the dough, think about it like a clock. Hold the bun in your left hand and, using your right, pinch the 12 o'clock to the 11, 10, 9, and so on until the edges are gathered back around to the starting position. While the right hand is gathering the edges up, the left hand is slowly turning the bun in a clockwise motion. If you have an excessive amount of dough on the top, don't be afraid to pinch it off.

Repeat with the other five balls, then press them all just a little bit to flatten the top and bottom. Cover and set aside.

Pour enough oil to half submerge the pies into a frying pan and place it over medium heat. Once hot, add the pies (you might need to do this in batches) and cook them for 4–5 minutes on each side until golden brown. Adjust the heat as necessary and if they are cooked on the outside but still raw inside, then wrap them in foil and bake them in the oven for a further 15 minutes at 350°F (180°C). Drain the pies on paper towels once cooked.

Once they are cool enough to handle but still hot, split one open and add a generous amount of the fish mint stuffing.

92

Breads and Doughs

Juntun Guo Kui

Numbing Meat Pies
Makes 8 pies

军屯锅盔

Within the spectrum of breads and doughs found in Chinese breakfasts, for me, the *guo kui* (锅盔) occupies a special sweet spot.

The literal translation of guo kui is "pot helmet," which comes from the heavy cast-iron pans traditionally used to make this variety of bread. They are historically described as one of the "Ten Oddities" from Shaanxi province, the full list reading like a hodgepodge of much-loved characteristics that define the people of the region as distinct from its neighbors. It is a region of people considered as spice obsessed, lovers of big noodles, who are emotionally insular yet love ear-piercingly loud classical opera and who prefer to squat rather than sit on a chair. Other regions and cities have their own list of oddities, too, but Shaanxi has some of the most famous and well loved.

The guo kui was at one point in history the size of a manhole cover, made to satisfy hearty appetites and soldiers, but over the centuries it has spread and evolved into an entire family of breads that range in style, filling, and production method, all under the same name.

This recipe is for the Juntun variety. It is stout, round, and fried. Imagine that instead of laminating a croissant with butter, you did it with pork and heavily seasoned it with a comical amount of numbing Sichuan pepper. It is crunchy, rich, and comforting, with a soft center, but then suddenly… electrifying.

Over the centuries, the category has spread to neighboring provinces. Some of my favorites include Ganzhou guo kui, which are thick in the middle with thinner edges, like a UFO, and are firm and chewy in texture, complete with radiating ridges that turn golden brown as they cook, and Qishan guo kui that look like giant rich tea cookies, dry and moisture-free, designed for long-distance travel.

This recipe is from one of my favorite restaurants in Chengdu, run by a very friendly woman. In the summer, the kitchen moves outside onto the street and in the colder months, into the back of the shop. Pair these breads with spicy noodles that are light on numbing Sichuan pepper to give you the best balance at breakfast time.

→

94

Juntun Guo Kui

1⅔ cups (200 g) all-purpose flour
1 teaspoon instant yeast
1½ teaspoons baking soda
A pinch of salt
½ cup (120 ml) lukewarm water
Neutral oil, for greasing and frying
White sesame seeds, to garnish (optional)

For the filling
2 tablespoons Shaoxing wine
3 scallions
1 thumb-sized piece of fresh root ginger
2 tablespoons water
7 oz (200 g) fatty ground pork (15% fat)
½ teaspoon ground cumin
1–2 tablespoons ground Sichuan pepper

First, prepare the filling. Put the Shaoxing wine, scallions, ginger, and water into a blender and blend to a smooth paste.

Scrape this into a bowl, then add the pork and mix thoroughly. Add the cumin and Sichuan pepper, mix again, then set aside for the flavors to mingle.

96   Put the flour, yeast, baking soda, and salt into a bowl, then add the water. Bring together into a smooth dough with your hands, then knead for 4–5 minutes until smooth and springy. Cover and leave to rest at room temperature for 30 minutes.

Meanwhile, preheat the oven to 350°F (180°C).

Weigh the dough and divide it into eight equal-sized pieces, then lightly oil your hands and roll each piece into a long oblong about 2–2½ in (5–6 cm) wide and 12–14 in (30–35 cm) long.

Next, weigh the pork mixture and divide it into 16 portions. Using your hands, smear the oblongs of dough with a portion of the pork mixture, then roll them up. Turn the rolls on their side and press down with your hand to create a spiraled bun like a snail.

Roll out each piece into an oblong again and repeat the process, smearing with the pork mixture and rolling it up, then pressing into a snail bun. At this point, you can press the bun into some sesame seeds if you are using them.

Finally, roll each bun out into a flatter and slightly larger circle. You want it to be around ½–¾ in (1.5–2 cm) thick.

Pour enough oil into a frying pan to shallow-fry the breads. Cook the pies over medium-low heat for 17–20 minutes, flipping regularly, until they have a deep golden crust. Transfer the pies to a baking sheet as you go.

Bake the pies in the oven for 10–12 minutes so that the center is fully cooked, then serve hot.

Sheng Jian Bao

生煎包

Pan-Fried Soup Buns
Makes 16 buns

The less internationally famous brother to the *xiao long bao* (小笼包), *sheng jian bao* (生煎包) are texturally far more complex than their siblings. They are comprised of a pork and soup filling inside a dough wrapper with a characteristically crisp bottom and steamed upper. It is important to note that when eating sheng jian bao, timing is key, as they are not made to order like XLB. Arrive minutes before a fresh batch is ready and you're in for a treat. Arrive at the end and you will wonder what all the fuss is about. Part of the ceremony is watching them being made behind a window in a giant cast-iron pan, turned with a pair of pliers and a handle made of cardboard.

Within the sheng jian bao category there are three key styles, with levels of qualitative expression within each.

First, there is the fully leavened dough version that you can find at Da Hu Chun in Shanghai. Personally, I find their locations ugly and their sheng jian bao doughy and unsatisfying. There are those who argue that this style is the original, and in fancy high-end restaurants, especially in Hong Kong, you will find this style, crusted with sesame seeds and served in dainty paper muffin cups. They are always lackluster. The Taiwanese chain Gaochi uses a sourdough starter, which in principle is the original method, but I find theirs horribly sour and again unbalanced.

The second type uses a totally unleavened dough. This style can be found at Xiao Yang's, a chain in Shanghai with many locations. These are the workhorse version, the dough thin enough to allow you to consume several portions, potentially with a side of noodles or soup. They are almost comically stuffed and explode with soup— first-timers are horrifically scalded.

The third version is somewhere in the middle, and it can be found at Dong Tai Xiang, a small chain in Shanghai. We lived closest to their Shaanxi Nan Lu location and I would visit every week like I was taking a religious pilgrimage. This is the version I would introduce visitors to as the best example, and what makes it even better is that their locations are open 24 hours. They also make one of the better Congyou Banmian (see page 26) in the city.

→

Sheng Jian Bao

For the dough
½ cup (110 ml) water
½ cup (110 ml) whole milk
¼ oz (7 g) envelope instant yeast
1 teaspoon granulated sugar
A pinch of salt
2¾ cups (330 g) strong white bread flour
Neutral oil, for frying

For the filling
14 oz (400 g) fatty ground pork (15% fat or more)
1¾ oz (50 g) bamboo shoots (canned or vacuum
    packed), finely chopped
⅓ cup (70 ml) water
1 tablespoon dried shrimp, finely chopped or
    ground in a mortar and pestle
1 tablespoon light soy sauce
1 tablespoon Shaoxing wine
A pinch of granulated sugar
A pinch of salt

To serve
Black sesame seeds
Finely chopped scallion
Zhenjiang vinegar

First, make the dough. Combine the water, milk,
yeast, sugar, and salt in a bowl and stir well until
dissolved.

Put the flour into a bowl or stand mixer fitted with
the dough hook attachment and add the wet
ingredients, then mix until you have a smooth
dough that comes away from the sides of the
bowl. Cover and leave to rise at room temperature
for 45–60 minutes, or until doubled in size

Meanwhile, prepare the filling. Combine all the
ingredients in a bowl, then use your hand in a
claw shape to mix the meat in one direction and
one direction only. This will help whip the protein
structure, creating a light and delicate texture.

Weigh the dough and divide it into 16 equal-sized
balls. Roll each ball into a disc about 2½ in (6 cm)
in diameter.

Place a generous amount of the filling in the
center of one of the dough discs and fold the
dough up around it. Then, either daintily pleat the
top or just smush it together. The pleated side will
go face down into the pan anyway, but more pleats
mean more surface area to become crispy.

Heat a little oil in a large frying pan over medium-
high heat. Add the bao and let them gently sizzle—
you don't want them to burn. Cook for 5–7 minutes
until golden brown on the bottom.

Meanwhile, boil a kettle of water. When the bao
are browned on the bottom, pour over the boiling
water until it is just less than halfway up the side
of the bao and cover with a lid. Continue to cook
for a further 10 minutes. Once the water has
been absorbed and the pan is looking dry again,
scatter over some black sesame seeds and finely
chopped scallion, then serve with Zhenjiang
vinegar for dipping.

Mantou

Steamed Breads
Makes 15–20 buns

Generally speaking, the north and west of China are much better at handling wheat flour and gluten than the south. There is a deftness with the hands across the northern stretch from Dongbei to Xinjiang that gives breads and baked goods a tenderness, flakiness, and certain mouthfeel that doesn't exist in Cantonese or Fujian cooking. The slippery, chewy, bouncy textures of rice-based dishes such as noodles, which are so expertly made in the south, are less desirable in bread and buns.

The steamed delights at the Gulou Mantou shop in Beijing are something of an internet sensation. Torn open, their *mantou* (馒头) have an internal composition that is rolled and folded with such attention to detail that they are both dense and delicate, their dough peeling off like layers of an onion.

In Shaoxing, at Jiu Niang Mantou, they use their own fermented rice wine as the starter to ferment the dough. The result is a perfumed and exquisitely light mantou. By far one of the lightest I have eaten, but with that elusive (and I feel necessary) skin, like a perfect summer peach. You can enjoy them as they are or ask for one split open and stuffed with chunks of red-braised pork or vegetables to be enjoyed in the courtyard garden with drying bamboo steamers stacked in rows.

By definition, a mantou is unfilled, but that doesn't stop certain areas from mixing things up. In the Shanghainese dialect, *sheng jian bao* (生煎包; see page 99) are sometimes listed as *sheng jian mantou* (生煎馒头). To every rule, there is always an exception. There is also a secondary level of inventiveness when it comes to mantou leftovers.

At Yue Bin Fan Guan in the Cui Hua Hutong in Beijing (the first restaurant to open after the Chinese Communist Revolution) they serve leftover mantou thickly sliced, dipped in egg, and fried. This is a classic way to use leftovers, usually as a side dish for lunch or dinner.

As part of dim sum or a sweet dish at dinner in Cantonese cooking, mantou are deep-fried until lightly golden brown and dipped into condensed milk while still incredibly hot. Dangerous and delicious.

In the city of Xi'an in Shaanxi province, mantou are baked rather than steamed, then toasted on both sides until golden brown. They are cut open and then given a brush of *tianmianjiang* and stuffed with plenty of julienned vegetables, such as carrots, potatoes, and pickled radishes. Optional extras are chile crisp and a fried egg.

Mi jiu (米酒) is a fermented rice wine with around 1 percent alcohol. The variety found in a jar with a cloudy appearance and pieces of rice floating in it is better than the distilled variety in a bottle. If you can't find it, just use 2½ cups (580 ml) water.

→

Mantou

2 cups (480 ml) mi jiu
Scant ½ cup (100 ml) water
¼ oz (7 g) envelope instant yeast
2½ teaspoons sugar
6 cups (750 g) cake or dumpling flour

Combine the mi jiu, water, yeast, and sugar in a
bowl and set aside for a minute to dissolve.

Put the flour into a bowl or stand mixer fitted with
the hook attachment and add the wet ingredients
while mixing on medium speed. Mix until you have
a smooth dough that comes away from the sides
of the bowl.

Scrape the dough down, then cover and leave
to rise at room temperature for 1 hour, or until
doubled in size.

Once risen, weigh the dough, then divide it into
either 15 or 20 equal-sized pieces.

Roll each piece into a ball, covering the balls with
plastic while you make and shape the rest.

104 Take one ball and roll it out on a clean surface into
an oval tongue shape about 12 in (30 cm) long
and 2 in (5 cm) wide. Roll it along the length, then
stand it up and press it down into a ball, shaping it
smooth. The shape should be almost spherical,
but don't be worried if it's slightly stout and flat or
cone-like. Repeat with the rest of the dough, then
leave to rise, covered with the plastic, for 30–40
minutes. They might not double in size, but they
will be lighter and bloated like the Michelin man.

Prepare a steamer and line the basket with
parchment paper with some holes poked in it.
Bring the water to a boil, then steam the buns, in
batches if necessary, for 15–20 minutes. They will
develop a skin, but the only way to really know if
they're ready is to split one open.

If you can't finish all the mantou, you can freeze
them after they have cooled and then re-steam
them from frozen for 5–7 minutes .

Hua Juan

花卷

Flower Buns

Makes 12–15 buns

The construction of these buns reminds me a lot of making Western cinnamon rolls. The dough is rolled out into a large, thin square, then a filling is added, and it is rolled up into a long sausage. The buns are cut and then a chopstick is pressed down the middle, causing the sides to splurge out. A small fold, tuck, and a pinch result in the flowering design.

When I was in the city of Shenzhen, I walked past a shop making these by the hundreds. Beyond the standard fillings of scallion and pork, they also had a "hot pot" version that was a combination of immensely spicy and sweet with a hint of sesame.

The aim here is to create as many layers, or "petals," for your flower as possible, so roll the dough out as thinly as you can. What you will also notice in the video is how wet, and thus spreadable, the pork filling is.

→

Hua Juan

1½ cups (350 ml) warm water
1 teaspoon granulated sugar
⅓ oz (10 g) fresh yeast or ¼ oz (7 g) envelope
    instant yeast
3¼ cups (400 g) strong white bread flour, plus
    extra for dusting
Neutral oil, for greasing

For a vegan filling
1½ tablespoons all-purpose flour
3½ tablespoons neutral oil
2 teaspoons ground white pepper
1 teaspoon salt
1 teaspoon Chinese five spice
1 teaspoon Chile Crisp (see page 282, or use
    store-bought) or chile paste (optional)
10 scallions, finely chopped

For a meaty filling
9 oz (250 g) ground pork
1½ tablespoons all-purpose flour
3½ tablespoons water
2 teaspoons ground white pepper
1 teaspoon salt
1 teaspoon Chile Crisp (see page 282, or use
    store-bought) or chile paste (optional)
10 scallions, finely chopped

Pour the water into a bowl, add the sugar and
yeast, and wait for it to bloom. Add the flour, then
bring it together into a smooth yet soft dough,
either with your hands or in a stand mixer fitted
with the dough hook attachment.

Knead the dough for 10 minutes by hand or
5 minutes in the stand mixer, then tip it out, oil the
bowl, and return the dough to the bowl. Cover and
leave to rise at room temperature for 1 hour, or
until doubled in size.

For the vegan filling, combine the flour and oil in a
bowl to make a paste. Add the white pepper, salt,
Chinese five spice, and chile, if using. Set aside.

For the meat filling, combine the pork, flour, and
water to make a wet paste. Add the white pepper,
salt, and chile, if using. Set aside.

Knock back the dough, then tip it out onto a large,
clean table lightly dusted with flour. Roll the dough
into a rectangle as large and as thin as you can.

Smear over your chosen filling in a thin, even layer.
Sprinkle over the scallions.

Starting from one of the long sides of the
rectangle, tightly roll it up into a long sausage.

Cut the sausage into pieces about 1½ in (4 cm).
Lay a chopstick lengthways on top of one piece
and press down so that the cut sides splurge out
a little, then pinch the edges together to hide the
smooth top with the chopstick indent. Repeat with
the remaining pieces.

Prepare a steamer and line the basket with
parchment paper with some holes poked in it,
then steam the buns for 15 minutes over medium-
high heat. Remove from the heat and leave the
buns to steam in the residual heat for a further
2–3 minutes.

Serve immediately or leave to cool entirely and
then freeze them. Re-steam from frozen for
10–12 minutes.

109

You Ta Zi

Steamed Oil Buns
Makes 6–8 buns

油塔子

These steamed buns are part of the unique trinity of breakfast items that I ate in Urumuqi, Xinjiang. Alongside a bowl of Umaaqi (see page 268) and a small dish of tangy Liangban Huang Luobo Si (see page 288), this completes the standard order for most mornings. At first glance, the buns look a lot like a regular *baozi* from Han Chinese cooking (see page 115), but after taking the first bite the entire thing unravels and the layers are revealed.

The key ingredient here is *jianshui* (碱水) or "alkali water," also known as lye water. This food-safe combination of potassium carbonate and sodium carbonate is used in China in various dishes, from Lanzhou hand-pulled noodles to Cantonese mooncakes, for its different properties. In typical bread-baking, for example, the yeast thrives in an acidic environment, which gives a complex crumb and crunchy crust. By raising the pH level with an alkalizing agent, such as lye water, the yeast is inhibited and the texture of the baked item changes. Think about pretzels or bagels after they have been in a lye bath, with their characteristic chewy texture and dark brown color. When making noodles, it gives incredible elasticity and a bouncy texture in the mouth.

In this recipe, the lye water means that instead of a brittle or tight dough, we get an elastic dough that can be stretched out to a great length and rolled up. An oiled surface and hands make light work of this process.

You can buy jianshui in all Chinese supermarkets or online with ease. Be careful not to use it too liberally, as it can create an unpleasant bitter aftertaste. Measure carefully, don't just splash it in!
→

You Ta Zi

2½ cups (300 g) all-purpose flour
Scant 1 cup (200 ml) water
1 teaspoon granulated sugar
2 tablespoons jianshui
¼ oz (7 g) envelope instant yeast
½ teaspoon salt
⅓ cup (80 ml) neutral oil
4 oz (120 g) rendered lamb fat (or lard, melted
    butter, or neutral oil)

To serve
Umaaqi (see page 268)
Liangban Huang Luobo Si (see page 288)

Put the flour, water, sugar, jianshui, yeast, and
salt into a bowl and bring together into a smooth
dough with your hands. Knead the dough for
10 minutes by hand or for 5 minutes in a stand
mixer, then cover and leave to rise at room
temperature for 1 hour, or until doubled in size.

Tip out the dough onto a clean surface and knead
for a minute, then divide it into six or eight pieces
depending how big you want your buns to be.

Roll each piece into a ball, then coat with a little of
the oil and cover with a tea towel or plastic. Leave
to rest for 15–20 minutes.

Smear some oil on your work surface and hands,
then flatten out one of the dough balls and
carefully and gently spread it thinner and longer.
You want to create a long noodle of dough around
2 in (5 cm) wide and 24–27 in (60–70 cm) long.

Take a teaspoon of the lamb fat (or any of the
alternatives if using) and spread it across the
length of the dough in a very thin layer. Roll the
dough up from one end to the other, keeping the
layers tight, until you have a short cylinder. Stand
it up and give it a press with the palm of your hand
until it is flattened a little but not flat like a pancake.
Repeat with the remaining dough.

Prepare a steamer and line the basket with
parchment paper with some holes poked in it,
then steam the buns for 17–20 minutes over a
roiling boil. They will lose their glossy oiliness and
become firm to the touch when ready. Serve with
the soup and carrot slaw.

112

Baozi 包子

Filled Steamed Buns

There are a million ways to make *baozi* (包子), in the same that way there are infinite minor permutations for making sourdough bread or instructions online for how to boil an egg perfectly. But, while the flavors and fillings are limitless, the dough is largely the same everywhere.

To some, it's a simple steamed bread that might be considered rather bland. A blank canvas for rich, salty, or sweet fillings, much like a bowl of white rice. For me, when someone says baozi I immediately think of two specific examples: the first is from a small shop on Wulumuqi Lu in Shanghai that we lived next to for some years. They made two fillings, a simple pork one with bamboo and ginger and another made from shepherd's purse dotted with tiny pieces of smoked tofu.

The second example I think of is my father making the Cantonese-style *char siu bao* that I grew up on. I was completely unaware that my Shanghainese grandfather preferred them to those from his home province. I learned about him from my aunt and grandmother, including how he traveled the world on the Blue Funnel Line and about his love for certain foods picked up along the journey from Shanghai to Liverpool.

For some people, the pleating of a bao can be scary, but truth be told, you don't have to pleat a bao closed. If it is simply too off-putting for you, just mush it closed and put the ugly side on the bottom. After a rest you'll have a luscious, smooth, moon-like bao. As long as its sealed, that's all that really matters. The communal gathering of friends and family for homemade bao is far more rewarding than the soulless perfection of a restaurant chain.

The type of filling you choose will dictate how much you fill the bao. Pork and bamboo as well as shepherd's purse and tofu are typically a generous tablespoon as these are breakfast staples eaten as a single item on the street. Red bean and liquid egg yolk are typically eaten as part of more complete meals, such as Cantonese-style dim sum, or as dessert. Since they are very rich in flavor, there is less filling and the baozi will be smaller.

To make the whitest bao, try sourcing bleached flour from your local Asian supermarket or flour that is labeled as specifically for bao. You can also buy (at least in China), food-grade bleach for bread flour, although I don't think many Westerners would go for it.

As with all filled items, it's best to weigh your filling and your dough and do some quick math. Having all your baozi the same size will not only look better, but will ensure they are all evenly cooked. Usually, a large bao will use 1¾ oz (50 g) uncooked dough and smaller bao will use around 1¼ oz (35 g).

With all bao recipes, steam over medium heat. After they have finished steaming, remove from the heat and leave the lid on for another minute. This will allow your buns to cool slightly and therefore avoid the risk of temperature shock, which can cause a wrinkly skinned bun.

→

Basic Baozi

Makes 8 large or 12 smaller buns

⅔ cups (150 ml) warm water
¼ oz (7 g) envelope instant yeast
2½ teaspoons granulated sugar
2½ cups (300 g) bleached strong white bread
   flour or all-purpose flour, plus extra for dusting
1½ teaspoons baking powder
1 tablespoon neutral oil
A pinch of salt
Baozi filling of your choice (see pages 118–19)

Combine the water, yeast, and sugar in a bowl and set aside for 10 minutes to dissolve.

Put the flour, baking powder, oil, and salt into a bowl or stand mixer and slowly add the wet ingredients until fully incorporated. Knead the dough for 10 minutes on medium speed or by hand for 15 minutes.

Roll the dough out on a lightly floured surface into a 12 x12 in (30 x 30 cm) square, then fold into thirds like a letter and repeat in the other direction until you have a square. Roll out again in one direction until you have a rectangle about 20–24 in (50–60 cm) long and 6 in (15 cm) wide. Finally, roll up the rectangle from one of the shorter sides to create a fat sausage.

Divide the sausage into eight pieces for large bao or 12 for small. Cover the pieces with plastic or a bowl while you roll them out.

Roll each dough ball into a 4–5 in (10–12 cm) diameter disc.

Next, fill the baozi with your chosen filling. The amount of filling you add will be dependent on the size of the baozi and the type of filling, but a good starting rule is to never overfill. The risk of causing a mess by being too generous is a far greater failure than being too frugal with the filling. Leftover filling can be chilled, frozen, or used creatively and if you run out of filling, extra dough can be steamed plain. Secondly, make sure you firmly seal your baozi closed.

When sealing the dough, think about it like a clock. Hold the bun in your left hand and, using your right, pinch the 12 o'clock to the 11, 10, 9, and so on until the edges are gathered back around to the starting position. While the right hand is gathering the edges up, the left hand is slowly turning the bun in a clockwise motion. If you have an excessive amount of dough on the top, don't be afraid to pinch it off.

Place each filled baozi into a steamer basket lined with parchment paper with some holes poked in it. Give them plenty of space to spread. Leave to rise at room temperature for 15–30 minutes. The size won't increase much, but it will give the gluten a moment to rest after being handled.

Prepare a steamer and cook the baozi for 10–12 minutes over a rolling boil until risen and the filling is cooked through. The skin will have a sheen to it and will be firm to the touch. Baozi can happily sit in a steamer for an hour over the lowest simmer, but they are certainly best when fresh.

117

Shepherd's Purse, Mushroom, and Tofu Filling

Makes enough for 8 large buns

Shepherd's purse is a green leaf loved by the Shanghainese. It's almost impossible to buy it fresh outside of China unless you grow it yourself, but you can find it in the freezer section at most Asian supermarkets. Its flavor is similar to rocket, so that's my suggestion for a good substitution.

118

1½ oz (40 g) dried chestnut mushrooms
10 dried wood ear mushrooms
5½ oz (150 g) shepherd's purse, wilted, then
    drained and finely chopped
1¾ oz (50 g) smoked tofu, finely chopped
½ teaspoon MSG
A pinch of salt
A pinch of granulated sugar

Put the mushrooms into a bowl and cover with boiling water. Set aside for 20 minutes to rehydrate.

Strain the mushrooms, reserving the liquid. This can be used as a base for many soups or can be reused to soak future batches of mushrooms to create a more intense broth.

Finely chop the mushrooms, then transfer to a bowl and add the rest of the ingredients.

Use the filling to make baozi following the instructions on page 117, using around 1½–1¾ oz (40–50 g) filling per baozi.

Xinjiang Pumpkin Filling

Makes enough for 8 large buns

These simple pumpkin-filled baozi were part of the breakfast spread I was served alongside the Qing Tang Mian on page 42.

14 oz (400 g) pumpkin, peeled and grated
3 tablespoons salt, plus extra to season
1 teaspoon granulated sugar
1 teaspoon sesame oil

Put the grated pumpkin into a bowl with the salt and set aside for 30 minutes to draw out the excess water that would otherwise make the baozi soggy.

Wash the pumpkin thoroughly and drain, then pat dry with paper towels or a tea towel.

Season with a pinch of salt, the sugar, and sesame oil and mix with your hands.

Use the filling to make baozi following the instructions on page 117, using around 1½–1¾ oz (40–50 g) filling per baozi.

Shanghai-Style Pork Filling

Makes enough for 8 large buns

A simple and fragrant baozi that has local variations across the country.

A thumb-sized piece of fresh root ginger
2 scallions
3½ tablespoons water
9 oz (250 g) fatty ground pork (15% fat—if using lean pork, add 1 tablespoon lard)
1 tablespoon light soy sauce
1 tablespoon dark soy sauce
1 tablespoon granulated sugar
1 tablespoon sesame oil
1 teaspoon ground white pepper
A pinch of salt

Put the ginger, scallions, and water into a food processor and blend until smooth, then pass through a sieve to remove any large pieces.

Add the rest of the ingredients to the food processor along with the ginger and scallion mixture and pulse for about 10–15 seconds until you have a smooth mixture.

Use the filling to make baozi following the instructions on page 117, using around 1½ oz (40 g) filling per baozi.

Red Bean Filling

Makes enough for 12 small buns

Red bean (*dousha*, 豆沙) is a polarizing flavor. You either adore it (often due to childhood memories), or you are faced with regret each time you bite into something thinking it might be chocolate only to realize that no, it was red bean, again.

119

Homemade red bean paste is incredibly laborious to make and requires at least 2 days of preparation. While no specialist equipment is technically needed, using some does yield better results. Using a machine with stone rollers rather than blades (similar to how Indians traditionally made rice batters or how the best hummus is made) will result in an exceptionally smooth paste.

If you want to make red bean baozi, I would recommend trying different store-bought varieties of red bean paste first and seeing which one you prefer, if you like it at all.

13 oz (360 g) red bean paste
Neutral oil, for greasing

With lightly oiled hands, divide the red bean paste into 1 oz (30 g) pieces and roll into balls.

Use the filling to make baozi following the instructions on page 117.

Doujiang Momo

豆浆馍馍

Steamed Soy Bean Cakes

Makes 12 cakes

The laid-back attitude that many Sichuanese have can be in part accredited to an ancient engineering project in the small town of Dujiangyan.

In 256 BCE, construction started on an artificial levee that would control the flow of the wild Min River. The devastating floods that had caused chaos across the region, destroying crops and killing thousands, suddenly came to an end and Sichuan became a land of plenty where its residents could focus on drinking tea and playing mahjong.

The levee itself is not much to see, but in the town of Dujiangyan there is a shop that has transformed a rather ordinary cake into something magical. *Doujiang momo* (豆浆馍馍) are made with soy beans, rice flour, and sugar—nothing too crazy. Fresh soy milk is made and left, unstrained, to ferment for two days. This is then mixed by hand in huge bowls with rice flour and sugar. Nothing is weighed, but simply measured with the eyes.

In the summer months, they use mulberry leaves to wrap the momo, delicately folding the parcels of batter into triangles that resemble Elven bread from *The Lord of the Rings*. In the winter, they use corn husks, using the corn for other recipes.

A great item to throw in your bag and take on the road, the cake is firm but spongey like an American pound cake and can withstand some rough handling.

Technically speaking, any cake batter can be steamed—even a Victoria sponge cake. A bamboo steamer works best as the steam is absorbed naturally into the material. With a glass lid, the moisture condenses and drips onto the food, causing imperfections.

If you can't source corn husks, then you can easily steam these in small ramekins or in a muffin pan if you have one that will fit into a steamer.

→

Doujiang Momo

Generous 1 cup (200 g) dried soy beans
Generous 2 cups (500 ml) water
¼ cup (50 g) granulated sugar
¼ oz (7 g) envelope instant yeast
Corn husks, for wrapping (available online from
    Mexican grocery stores)
1½ cups (200 g) rice flour

Put the soy beans into a bowl, cover with water, and leave to soak overnight, or for at least 8 hours. Once they are soft enough to break between two fingers, discard the water and transfer the beans to a blender.

Add the measured water and blend until smooth—the consistency should be like pancake batter.

Pour the soy batter into a saucepan and cook it over medium heat for 10–15 minutes, stirring constantly with a spatula to make sure it doesn't catch on the bottom of the pan. The purpose here is to remove the intense raw bean flavor.

Pour the batter into a bowl and add 1 teaspoon of the sugar, then leave to cool completely.

Once cool, stir in the yeast, then cover with a cloth and leave to rest overnight, or for at least 12 hours.

Soak the corn husks in boiling water for 15–20 minutes to soften them up. Make sure they are fully submerged—you can weigh them down with a small plate or bowl.

Add the rice flour and the remaining sugar to the soy batter and stir thoroughly to combine. In Sichuan they use their hands, but a spatula will work the same. The consistency will be like buttery mashed potato.

Now fill the corn husks. You might need to overlap two if they are too skinny. Dollop 3–4 tablespoons of the batter onto the corn husk just below the center.

Fold the bottom left corner up towards the 3 o'clock position, to create a point at the bottom. Then take the bottom right corner and fold it up to the 9 o'clock position to make a cone. Fold over the top to the middle and flip the whole thing over. You should have a handsome triangular parcel that looks a little like a samosa. Repeat with the remaining batter.

Place the parcels in a steamer basket lined with parchment paper with some holes poked in it, resting them against each other as if they're dragon's scales.

Steam the parcels over high heat for 17–20 minutes until firm to the touch. Remove from the heat and leave them to rest for a further 3–4 minutes in the residual heat.

Peel and serve.

Breads and Doughs

Shaobing 烧饼

Flaky Baked Breads
Makes 8 breads

Literally a "baked cake," the *shaobing* (烧饼) is a celebration of flaky, crisp simplicity in the same way that a croissant is in its neutral form. In Shanghai, it is a simple street food that is baked in a tandoor oven, which is a fuel-efficient method for cooking several batches at once. Grab one to go and dip it in some freshly made *doujiang* (豆浆), soy milk that can be served sweet or savory, or split it open and stuff it with thinly sliced donkey meat and fresh, crunchy chile pepper for a Hebei breakfast (see opposite).

Shaobing are usually studded with a mass of sesame seeds, which are a useful indicator in the cooking process, too. They help to make sure your heat isn't too high and you don't overcook your bing—if the sesame seeds are burning, you'll know. In Beijing, they can also be laced with fennel seeds that impart a pungent liquorice flavor, but in this case, they are a side dish for the lamb hotpots popular during the freezing winters rather than a breakfast item. The thinner you roll the shaobing, the crisper they will be; the fatter you leave them, the more distinct layers of dough they will reveal.

3 cups (350 g) all-purpose flour, plus 1 tablespoon for the spice paste and extra for dusting
¼ oz (7 g) envelope instant yeast
½ teaspoon salt, plus a pinch
Scant 1 cup (200 ml) warm water, or as needed
2 scallions, thinly sliced
½ teaspoon Chinese five spice
½ teaspoon granulated sugar
Scant 1 cup (200 ml) vegetable or sunflower oil, plus extra for frying
1 cup (150 g) white sesame seeds

Combine the flour, yeast, and the pinch of salt in a bowl or stand mixer fitted with the dough hook attachment, then slowly add enough water to create a firm dough. Knead for 10 minutes in the mixer or for 20 minutes by hand until the dough is smooth. Cover and leave to rest at room temperature for 20 minutes.

Preheat the oven to 350°F (180°C).

In a small heatproof bowl, stir together the tablespoon of flour with the scallions, Chinese five spice, remaining salt, and the sugar. Heat the oil in a small saucepan over high heat until almost smoking, then pour it over the flour mixture in small dribbles. It will sizzle furiously. Stir well to create a smooth paste, then set aside.

Roll out the dough on a lightly floured surface into a 20–24 in (50–60 cm) square, then generously brush the surface with the spice paste. Roll the dough up tightly into a long sausage, then cut it into eight equal-sized pieces.

Take one piece of dough and pinch the open edges closed. Press it flat, then fold it in half. Pinch it around the edges again. Shape it into a circle, then repeat with the remaining dough pieces.

Tip the sesame seeds onto a small plate or bowl and pour a little water into another dish. Dip one side of the bread into the water and then press it into the sesame seeds—you want a lot of seeds! Press the buns flat or use a rolling pin to roll them out into small ovals, about 8 x 3½ in (20 x 9 cm).

Heat a little oil in a frying pan over low-medium heat and fry the shaobing on both sides for 7–8 minutes until the sesame seeds are golden brown.

Once fried, transfer them to a baking sheet and bake in the oven for 10 minutes. Remove from the oven and allow to cool slightly before serving.

Lü Rou Huo Shao

驴
肉
火
烧

Donkey Meat Sandwiches
Makes 4 sandwiches

The origins of Hebei's donkey sandwiches are unclear, but in my opinion it's important when eating dishes like this to remember that many cultures have experienced difficult periods and necessary sacrifices were made by our ancestors in order to survive. Rarely do societies eat their working animals unless faced with some sort of extreme famine or poverty. That being said, while donkey meat might sound unusual, for many continental Europeans who eat horse regularly this won't be too unfamiliar in flavor or texture. The quote overleaf suggests that the second-best choice is still sometimes a good alternative—donkey meat is delicious and not necessarily a last resort.

There are two key types of donkey meat sandwich: a round version from Baoding that is made with hot meat and a rectangular sandwich from Hejian that is made with cold meat.

The first time I tried this (the Baoding version) I was in Beijing for work and I had it served at breakfast with a hard-boiled egg and a bowl of scalding-hot egg drop soup.

The meat is roughly chopped with green chiles, similar to the type you would find in Turkish cuisine. It is fresh and peppery with only a mild kick. The bread is wonderfully flaky but soft, like a cross between a croissant and a ciabatta.

Texturally, the meat is similar to the salt beef you find in an East London bagel shop. In the US and UK, the taboo around eating horsemeat extends to donkey, too. The best substitute is a cut of beef bottom round or brisket for a rich flavor.

In Northeast China it's not uncommon to simply purchase a piece of ready-cooked donkey meat at a delicatessen or supermarket in the same way you might buy a rotisserie chicken.

125

Lü Rou Huo Shao

3 lb 5 oz (1.5 kg) beef bottom round or brisket
1 cup (250 ml) light soy sauce
⅓ cup (70 g) granulated sugar
1½ teaspoons table salt
3 bay leaves
½ x quantity Shaobing dough (see page 124;
    omit the sesame seeds and scallion if
    you prefer)
4 mild long green chiles, deseeded and
    finely chopped
4 handfuls of cilantro, chopped

First, prepare the beef. Put the beef into a large
pot and cover with water. Set aside to soak for 1
hour, then discard the water and replace with just
enough to cover the meat. Add the soy sauce,
sugar, salt, and bay leaves.

Bring to a boil, then reduce the heat to low. Cover
and cook for 4–6 hours until the meat is soft and
pulls apart easily with a fork.

Divide the shaobing dough into four pieces and,
depending on how you want to eat your sandwich
(hot or cold), shape the pieces into rounds or
rectangles.

Cook the shaobing according to the instructions
on page 124, then leave them to cool slightly while
you prepare the filling.

If you're making the Baoding (hot) version, reheat
the shredded or chopped meat in a dry frying pan
or microwave. If you are eating it Hejian style, then
your work is already done.

Put the meat, chiles, and cilantro into a bowl and
stir to combine, then use it to stuff the breads.

This recipe makes more meat than you'll need—
leftovers can be frozen for later use or diced up
and used in any recipes that require chopped
meat, such as Lawei Nuomi Fan (see page 170).

天上龙肉，地上驴肉

*"In the heavens there is dragon meat,
and on Earth there is donkey meat."*

Xizhou Baba

Xizhou-Style Breakfast Breads

Makes 4 breads

喜洲粑粑

The town of Xizhou, Yunnan, has seen something of a renaissance over recent years. It has become an enclave of artists, poets, filmmakers, and inventive chefs seeking refuge from the larger Chinese cities in the east. The new pour-over coffee shops and natural wine bars complement one of the most delicious and traditional items you can find on the street, the Xizhou version of the *baba* (粑粑).

However, unlike the simple fried dough like that served at Miao Lu (see page 70), here the baba is made in a similar way to the Shanghainese Congyou Bing (see page 82). The fluffy pizza dough-like bread is layered with lard as if you were making a croissant or puff pastry. It is then studded with ground pork, topped with a cracked egg, and then cooked on a large hot plate that is covered with a lid on a suspended arm, which is topped with glowing charcoal. Particularly interesting is the way in which the baba is momentarily launched into the air with a flick of the wrist before falling into the pan.

This dish really checks a lot of boxes when it comes to satisfying a hangover—crisp, flaky, doughy carbs combined with salty pork and protein from the egg, and the whole thing not too large that you get bored of it but definitely generous enough that you're not going to be left hungry when you finish.

1 x quantity Baba dough (see page 70)
1 cup (200 g) lard
5½ oz (150 g) ground pork
2 scallions, finely chopped
4 eggs
Salt and black pepper

Preheat the oven to 425°F (220°C). You can use a pizza oven for this if you have one.

Divide the baba dough into four pieces and press each one out with your hands into a circle the size of a dinner plate. Place the dough on a piece of parchment paper.

With your hands, smear 2 tablespoons of the lard across the middle of each baba, then top with ground pork and some scallion, and season generously with salt and pepper. Fold the edges into the middle, sealing in the lard and pork, then shape them into 6–7 in (15–17 cm) circles.

With a knife, make a cut in the middle to allow the air to escape.

Heat the remaining lard in a small saucepan until melted.

Bake the babas in the oven for 8 minutes, then brush them with some of the melted lard. Flip them over, brush with more lard and bake for a further 8 minutes until starting to brown. Crack an egg on top of each baba and break the yolk, smearing it across the surface. Season the egg with extra salt and pepper. Return it to the oven for a further 8 minutes until golden brown and puffy.

Remove from the oven and cut each into six pieces before serving.

Breads and Doughs

Kao Nang 烤馕
نان

Spiced Flatbreads
Makes 4 breads

China's Muslim population is largely spread throughout Xinjiang, Shaanxi, Qinghai, and Gansu provinces, collectively known as the Xibei (northwest) region. In the homes and street markets of these areas you will inevitably encounter stacks of circular breads called *nang* (馕). In appearance these breads are not dissimilar to pizza bases, but with a heavy tan and decorated with beautiful, intricate designs made with a special tool. Today, these tools are mostly metal, but some traditional examples are made with feathers (see overleaf).

Perhaps unsurprisingly, the word nang is derived from the bread's cousin from the Indian subcontinent, naan. They come in a wide spectrum of sizes. The smallest, just the size of a coin, is called *tokashi*, while the largest, the size of a car steering wheel, is called *emanke*.

Most nang are plain, but some are flavored or stuffed with rose petals, sesame seeds, or lamb, while others are made with buckwheat rather than wheat flour.

The *wowo nang* (窝窝馕) from Kashgar is similar to a bagel in shape but is not boiled before baking.

Nang are eaten throughout the day, cut into salads, ripped into chunks and added to soups, consumed a nibble at a time, fried in lamb fat with peppers... the list goes on and on. They are repurposed in multiple other recipes throughout the day across the Xibei region and their versatility reminds me of how the Han Chinese in the east incorporate *youtiao* in numerous other dishes.

Typically, the breads are made in a tandoor, but a conventional oven does the job. This recipe includes a special spice blend, Chinese 13 spice, that you can find in almost any Asian supermarket, and a glaze of onion-infused oil that can also be used as a finishing oil for noodles, soups, or salads.

→

130

Kao Nang

1¼ cups (300 ml) neutral oil
1 large red or white onion, thinly sliced
5 cups (600 g) all-purpose flour, plus extra
   for dusting
1¼ cups (300 ml) whole milk
1 egg
1½ tablespoons granulated sugar
¼ oz (7 g) envelope instant yeast
1 teaspoon Chinese 13 spice
A pinch of salt
½ teaspoon ground white pepper
⅔ cup (100 g) white sesame seeds

Pour the oil into a deep frying pan or pot and add the onion. Cook over low heat for 15 minutes until the onion is golden brown, being careful not to let it burn. You want to do this slowly in order to extract as much flavor as possible. Remove from the heat and set aside to cool completely, leaving the onions in the oil. You can store this in the fridge for up to 10 days as long as the oil completely covers the onions.

For the nang dough, combine all the ingredients, except the sesame seeds, in a stand mixer fitted with the dough hook attachment. Mix until you have a smooth dough that comes away from the sides of the bowl, then cover and leave to rise at room temperature for 1 hour, or until doubled in size. It is possible to do this by hand, too, with some elbow grease.

Meanwhile, preheat the oven to 425°F (220°C).

Once risen, tip the dough out onto a clean surface and knead it by hand for 5 minutes.

Weigh the dough and divide it into four equal-sized pieces.

Roll one of the pieces into a ball, then roll it out on a lightly floured surface into a circle about 8–9 in (20–23 cm) in diameter. Use your hands to press it from the center to the edge, stretching it out to about 10 in (25 cm) across, with a thick edge and thinner center much like a pizza.

Transfer the nang to a baking sheet, then use a fork (or a special nang needle if you have one) to cover the center of the nang with holes. This will ensure the center remains flat when baking and does not warp. I would use this opportunity to be inventive with making a pretty pattern.

Spray or brush the surface of the nang with water, then liberally sprinkle with sesame seeds.

Bake in the oven for 12–15 minutes until it has a deep golden brown color. You may need to turn it for an even color. Keep an eye on it and if it is browning too quickly, cover with foil for the last few minutes so that it cooks properly but the sesame seeds do not burn.

Remove the nang from the oven and brush it liberally with the onion oil while hot. Repeat with the remaining dough.

Serve the nangs warm once cooked.

Kao Baozi

烤包子

سامسا

Xinjiang-Style Baked Lamb Buns
Makes 6–8 buns

These baked buns are also called *samusa* (سامسا) in the Uyghur language, which gives you a clue to their construction and style. Filled with fatty lamb or mutton, they have a melting texture and luscious taste. The meat's rich, robust, and gamey flavor is cut with an equal amount of onion and the mixture is spiced with cumin and lots of black pepper. They are baked in a tandoor oven at incredible temperatures—unfortunately beyond what most domestic appliances can reach. An egg wash will help to achieve that intense golden brown color.

There is no limit to what time of day you can eat these buns, from early morning, as a daytime snack, or even late at night at a street market. They are great to travel with, too, and are delicious hot or cold.

7 oz (200 g) lamb leg, diced
7 oz (200 g) onion, diced
1 tablespoon ground black pepper
2 teaspoons cumin seeds, toasted and ground, or ground cumin
2 teaspoons sesame oil
2½ cups (300 g) strong white bread flour, plus extra for dusting
2 teaspoons salt
2 eggs
⅔ cup (160 ml) warm water
White or black sesame seeds, to garnish (optional)

First, prepare the filling. This can be done the day before and stored, covered, in the fridge for the flavors to mix.

Using a cleaver or heavy knife, roughly mince the meat. You don't want a smooth paste. Transfer the meat to a bowl.

Add the onion along with the black pepper and cumin. Add a few splashes of water and the sesame oil and give everything a good mix. Cover and set aside.

To prepare the dough, put the flour and salt into a bowl. Beat one of the eggs into the water and slowly add it to the dry ingredients until a rough dough is formed. Press it together with your hands until you have a firm and smooth dough.

Cover and leave the dough to rest at room temperature for 30 minutes. You can also make the dough the day before and store it in the fridge, just remember to allow the dough to return to room temperature first before rolling.

Weigh and divide the dough into six or eight equal-sized pieces depending how big you want your kao baozi.

Roll each piece into a ball, then cover and leave to rest for a further 15 minutes.

Meanwhile, preheat the oven to 425°F (220°C).

Roll out one of the dough balls on a lightly floured surface into a thin circle 5–5½ in (12–14 cm) in diameter, then place a generous spoonful of the lamb mixture in the middle.

Fold the left and right side into the middle and seal with a dab of water, then fold the top and bottom to the middle to create a square or rectangular parcel. Repeat with the remaining dough and filling.

Place the kao baozi on a baking sheet with the folds facing down. Beat the remaining egg and use it to brush the kao baozi.

Sprinkle with sesame seeds, if using, then bake in the oven for 15 minutes until deep golden brown.

Remove from the oven and leave to cool for a few minutes before eating.

梅花蛋糕

Mei Hua Dan Gao

Plum Blossom Cakes

Makes 8–10 cakes

In the Sichuan countryside, a tiny house exists that makes a very simple yet delicious cake. In a large, flat pan, perhaps fifty individual molds are oiled and a simple, custardy batter is ladled precisely into each. The action begins when a single man angles what appears to be a mass of smoldering charcoal suspended on chains over the cakes, gently maneuvering the pendulous fire for even heat distribution. Throughout the cooking he checks the progress and, using small circles of foil, covers the areas that are coloring too quickly. The experience is certainly theatrical, but what seems so odd about this method of cooking is its apparent inefficiency.

The cakes go by a few rather uninteresting names, including *xian kao cai zi gao* (现烤槽子糕), literally "a freshly baked cake with a molded design," and *mei hua dan gao* (梅花蛋糕), "plum blossom cake," but none of them accurately describe the cakes' incredible production. I would prefer something like "inferno cakes"—a name that suggests the sense of impending doom and danger that was present in the room when I was watching them being made.

Many customers visit the tiny house to buy the cakes—some even purchase an entire pan of fluffy, buttery buns. When I was there,

the chatter often dropped to total silence as we all watched the master at work in awe. Most of the time he keeps his eyes closed because of the sheer amount of smoke produced.

The cakes are made by a husband-and-wife team. The husband starts his day at around 7 a.m. and he works until just after lunchtime. His wife prepares batches of batter with a high percentage of egg yolk, giving the cakes their golden color and distinctive, crowned top. The cakes are not a typical Sichuan breakfast, but they become one by default as the waiting customers are given freebies and, on leaving with their goods, consume another three or four as they walk back to their car. The rest are eaten with tea along with other snacks like nuts and dried fruit.

For those that have a pizza oven, replicating this will be relatively simple. Otherwise, bake the cakes in a muffin pan in a very hot oven.

3 eggs
1 egg yolk
⅓ cup (70 g) granulated sugar
2 tablespoons runny honey
3½ tablespoons neutral oil
scant 1 cup (100 g) all-purpose flour
1 teaspoon baking powder

Preheat your oven to 425°F (220°C).

Combine the eggs, egg yolk, sugar, honey, and oil in a bowl, then use an electric mixer to blend them until you have a pale yellow, foamy mixture. Start on a low speed to begin with.

Sift together the flour and baking powder, then gently fold this into the wet ingredients until just combined into a smooth batter. Be careful not to overmix.

Pour the batter into a muffin pan, filling the holes about two-thirds full, then bake in the oven for 15 minutes or until a skewer inserted into the center comes out clean.

137

Breads and Doughs

Breads and Doughs

Yuni Bing

Deep-Fried, Taro-Filled Cookie Sandwiches
Makes 10–12 sandwiches

With some species of taro, simply handling them raw can cause skin irritations, so it's best to wear kitchen gloves when preparing them and be careful not to touch your eyes. Do not eat any of the taro plant raw, especially the leaves.

3 lb 5 oz (1.5 kg) taro, peeled and cubed
2–4 tablespoons granulated sugar (depending on how sweet you like it)
1–2 x 10½ oz (300 g) packages of rich tea or digestive cookies
2 tablespoons all-purpose flour
1 tablespoon rice flour
⅔ cup (100 g) white sesame seeds (optional)
Neutral oil, for frying

Taro, often mistranslated as yam, is a traditional breakfast or snack in the southern Min area of Fujian. Usually it is peeled, steamed, and mashed, then flavored and sweetened with dried fruits and nuts before being smoothed into small, shallow bowls in which it is steamed again. The color varies from a light, dusty pink, to zombie grey.

While this fits the bill when we consider the traditional methods and presentation aesthetics of Chinese food, it is a far cry from the contemporary uses of taro in sweets, ice cream, bubble tea, and more. These developments are often dismissed as passing trends, partially because there is a strong nostalgia culture in China, especially when it comes to food and restaurant interiors.

But if you take the steamed taro and sandwich it between two rich tea cookies (sold in China as *zao cha bing* 早茶饼 or "morning tea biscuit") and then deep-fry it, you can see how something very ordinary can become both a marketable trend and an evolution of tradition. I think these cookie sandwiches are absolutely delicious, either as a side dish with the Huasheng Tang from page 265 or as an all-day treat with a cup of tea.

Prepare a steamer, then steam the taro over high heat for 17–20 minutes until fork-tender. Transfer the taro to a bowl and mash it. Add the sugar and combine, then set aside to cool.

Spread some of the mashed taro onto one of the cookies until it is about ½ in (1.5 cm) thick, then top with another biscuit to make a sandwich. Make sure the taro comes all the way to the edges and is smooth. Repeat with the remaining taro and cookies.

Combine the plain and rice flours with a few tablespoons of water in a bowl to create a thick paste. Using a pastry brush, coat the sides of the cookies in the batter to seal in the taro. Roll the edges in sesame seeds, if using.

Heat a 2 in (5 cm) depth of oil in a large pot, deep frying pan, or wok until it reaches 350°F (180°C).

Carefully add a few of the sandwiches to the hot oil, being careful not to overcrowd the pan. Fry for 2 minutes on each side each until golden brown, then drain on a wire rack or paper towels.

Repeat with the remaining sandwiches, then serve warm.

140

芋泥饼

Wugu Zaliang Rice and Other Grains

One of my favorite breakfast memories from China is from a trip I took with my sister in 2009 to climb Mount Emei in Sichuan. It is one of the five sacred Buddhist mountains of China and is a famous pilgrimage, with various temple stays along the route. I wasn't aware until that morning that we were set to embark on a two-day hike, and I was not happy or prepared. On the second day, we woke before sunrise, using our phones to light the path in pitch darkness. Eventually, we stopped for breakfast at a small shack that served only egg fried rice and we ate with abandon, washing it all down with a Coke for the pure sugar energy. It was more of a novelty to have a Coke for breakfast than anything else.

While rice is often grandly dubbed "the grain of life," variety will always be the spice. There are many cultures that rely on rice for food, but none like China treat it with such profound, almost spiritual reverence. The Chinese character *qi* (氣, or 气 in simplified Mandarin), which represents the vital energy that gives everything life, contains the character for rice in its construction. Beyond the idioms and intangible cultural signifiers it has, rice has been found mixed into the cement of the Great Wall, as a dye resist in fabrics, embedded in porcelain, and is even used medicinally. But before rice, there was the successful domestication of millet, *xiaomi* (小米), which sustained early kingdoms and tribes. Today, it's most commonly consumed as a porridge, Xiaomi Zhou (see page 144), or as a crunchy topping for salty Xinjiang milk tea (see page 178).

As a rather curious sidenote, I can't recall ever having eaten a bowl of plain, steamed white rice for breakfast anywhere in China. This kind of serving is usually reserved for lunch or dinner, when the table is full of other dishes. The leftovers are then repurposed for breakfast the next day, either for Paofan (see page 152) or, as I had halfway up a mountain in Sichuan, as a delicious egg fried rice.

Xiaomi Zhou

小米粥

Millet Porridge

Serves 3–4

In 1999, an archaeological dig near the town of Lajia in Northwestern China found evidence of a late Neolithic site. A sealed bowl was found within the site, containing 4,000-year-old preserved noodles made from millet. Further analysis discovered that the millet had been processed in a way that allowed the dough to be pulled rather than cut. Domesticated millet existed centuries before rice and wheat in China and this discovery demonstrated that the ancient communities of this region were already eating noodles as part of a regular diet.

Even if this recipe is a little simple—just millet and water—I enjoy eating it occasionally purely because of this discovery. I had this at the breakfast market in Qingdao one freezing-cold morning, served plain with no pickles or flavorings, but with two types of *youtiao*, one vegan and the other made with milk powder. Another time, on a car ride through Xinjiang, I had it barely sweetened in a takeout cup with a straw. Otherwise, it is typically served plain with other dishes like *baozi* or *jiaozi* on the side.

Zhou (粥), or congee as the Western world better knows it (from the Tamil *kanji*), comes in a variety of thicknesses and flavors and, most importantly, it is not always made with rice, as this recipe demonstrates. The recipe below makes a porridge that has the consistency of a thin soup, but you can add more water to create something more like a drink, similar to what I had in Xinjiang.

½ cup (100 g) millet
5½ cups (1.3 liters) water
1–2 tablespoons granulated sugar (optional)

Washing millet doesn't require the same agitation as rice. Put the millet into a bowl, cover with water, then carefully drain. Once is enough.

Pour the water into a saucepan and bring to a boil. Add the millet and sugar, if using, and cook over medium heat, stirring continuously, for 5 minutes.

Partially cover with a lid and reduce to a low simmer. Cook for a further 15 minutes, stirring occasionally, until the millet is tender. Remove from the heat. The porridge will thicken as it cools.

Miancha

Millet Porridge with Sweet Sesame
Serves 1

Long before I lived in China, my sister lived in Beijing, and for a time it was a city I knew much better than my ancestral home of Shanghai. In the unassuming residential compound in Chaoyang where she lived there was only one other foreign neighbor, an extraordinarily tall Dutch man who had an enormous pot-bellied pig as a pet. The Chinese neighbors were delighted and confused in equal measure.

I often visited my sister during the depths of the miserable Beijing winters, when the air was so dry that it chapped your lips. On these occasions, we would walk to a nearby street for breakfast, where we would visit toasty canteens that were lingering hangovers from the Communist era of social dining. I remember bright orange dinner trays, like you would get in a school canteen, with different sections for fried dumplings, dough sticks, and *miancha* (面茶). The literal translation for miancha is "flour tea." Neither are present in this dish. Instead, it is a gruel made with millet and topped with deeply toasted Chinese sesame paste that is lightly sweetened. The consistency is something between a soup and porridge, allowing you to slurp from the edge of the bowl before finishing the portion with a spoon. It is favored by the older generation for its ease of digestion and high fiber, being gentle both on the teeth and the bowels.

Paired with a Jiao Quan (see page 89), a crispy fried dough ring, it makes a perfect breakfast.

1¾ oz (50 g) Chinese sesame paste
2 tablespoons sesame oil
3½ tablespoons boiling water
1 teaspoon granulated sugar
¼ cup (60 g) millet, washed (see page 144)
½–⅔ cup (120–150 ml) cold water
Toasted sesame seeds, to garnish

Put the sesame paste and oil into a bowl and pour over the boiling water, then stir until a smooth paste is formed. Add more boiling water if necessary to create a smooth, pourable consistency. Stir in the sugar and set aside.

Combine the millet and cold water in a saucepan over medium heat and bring to a gentle simmer. Cook for 3–4 minutes, stirring regularly, until you feel it starting to thicken.

Pour some boiling water into a bowl to warm it, then discard the water. This is what they do in Beijing during the winter.

Transfer the miancha to the bowl and top with the sesame paste, then garnish with a sprinkling of sesame seeds. Serve hot.

Ersi and Erkuai

饵丝

Yunnan Rice Cakes

Serves 2–3

If you stay at the Linden center in Xizhou, Yunnan, and go on their morning market tour, you'll be taken to a small factory that makes rice cakes. In this steamy wonderland, they produce handmade *ersi* (饵丝) and *erkuai* (耳快). The former are cut into thin noodles or long sticks and are mostly used in soups, while the latter can be made in various shapes but are usually large pancakes that are fried or grilled or chunky ingots (see page 150) that can be cut at home into any desired shape and stir-fried with vegetables. The circles are often dry-fried until golden brown and filled with a sweet-savory sauce, *youtiao*, and pickles, as a sort of breakfast wrap.

Importantly, the rice used here is not the sticky variety. It is left to soak for several hours before being steamed in large vats with conical hats. While it is still hot, it is shoveled into what looks like a meat grinder, from which squiggly worms emerge. The bundles are thrown back into the grinder three times. Finally, a long, white sausage of rice dough appears. The consistency is bouncy and stretchy like chewing gum.

The dough is then pressed through rollers much like giant sheets of egg pasta. The rollers are lubricated with large pieces

of beeswax to keep everything moving smoothly. From there, it's up to the customer or chef how they wish to shape it, either into noodles or random slivers.

The result is a delightfully chewy texture with a naturally sweet flavor. At a restaurant in Jianchuan that I visited, they served it in a spectacular corn and pork broth topped with a huge variety of toppings: crispy tofu pieces, potato, pickles, thinly sliced omelet, scallions, and more (see page 54).

Dried ersi noodles are readily available outside of China, but dried erkuai is another story. If you want to give this a try at home, those lucky enough to have a meat-grinding attachment for their stand mixer are in with the best chance, but a food processor takes second place and is also the most practical option for most. Work with the rice while it is still hot from the steamer and don't stop until the consistency is stretchy like chewing gum.

149

Ersi and Erkuai

1½ cups (300 g) short-grain rice
Rice flour, for dusting

Put the rice into a bowl, cover with water, and leave to soak for at least 6 hours, or overnight.

Prepare a large steamer and line the basket with cheesecloth. Discard the soaking water and transfer the rice to the steamer, then cook for 15–18 minutes or until the rice is tender.

Quickly transfer the hot rice to a food processor and blend for about 5 minutes until you have a smooth white rice dough.

Remove the rice from the food processor and, while it is hot, manipulate it into whatever shape you like. A pasta machine makes light work of turning it into sheets of even thickness but a rolling pin will work, too. Roll the dough out on a surface lightly dusted with rice flour to prevent sticking. You're look for a thickness of ⅛–¼ in (3–5 mm).

Lay the sheets on clean tea towels and leave them to cool. You can cut the sheets into noodles for ersi or large circles for erkuai.

These are best enjoyed on the day of preparation but will freeze well for 2–3 months.

151

Paofan

Leftover Rice Soup
Serves as many as you like

There's nothing excessive or spectacular about a bowl of *paofan* (泡饭). It's quite simply leftover rice, cooked (or just reheated) in water, stock, or soup and then garnished with the leftovers from dinner the night before or something simple and elegant like sharp pickles or wilted green vegetables.

What paofan absolutely is not, is *zhou* (粥), aka congee. Congee is an art; a fine line between something perfectly rendered and layered in texture and something gone wrong that is gluey and incoherent.

The merits of making paofan are in its economical use of scraps to create a low-effort and not-half-bad finished dish. There are countless family and regional variations of this dish, so it's almost impossible to say that one encounter is representative of a particular place. Every time you make paofan it can be completely unique.

As always with leftover rice, there is a high risk of food poisoning. Rice should be refrigerated as soon as possible after you have finished eating and consumed within 24 hours. The spores of *Bacillus cereus* can survive incredibly high temperatures so no amount of heat will prevent you from getting sick. If in doubt, throw it out.

Boiling water, stock, or leftover soup, to cover
Leftover rice (whatever quantity you have)
Leftovers from your fridge, such as wilted vegetables, any protein, pickles, salted duck eggs, a leftover youtiao cut into pieces and toasted
Lard
Salt and white pepper

Pour the water, stock, or soup into a pot and bring to a gentle boil.

Add the rice and cook for 8–10 minutes. You want some of the rice grains to break down a little, but not too much.

Add your leftovers, season with the lard, salt, and white pepper and enjoy.

Nan Gua Zhou

南瓜粥

Pumpkin Congee
Serves 3–4

If there is one recurring theme in Chinese cuisine, it's balance. That goes for cooking and for eating. If you've eaten too much of something hot or "dynamic," you should consume something cooling to counteract that. Flavors are linked to specific organs that nourish them, too: sour for the liver, sweetness for the spleen, salt for the kidneys, bitterness for the heart, and spicy heat for the lungs. So, for example, while soy beans are cooling, peanuts provide us with hot energy, and chile can drive out dampness from the body, keeping our lungs free of mucus. There is also a third category of neutral foods that have no impact on the body's *qi* (气), and this includes white rice. Incidentally, I was once told off by a lovely follower on Instagram for eating watermelon with soy milk, as both are categorized as cooling, so it could have led to a reduction in my energy levels and a diminished vigor.

It is therefore of the utmost importance to keep your humors in balance. One way of doing this is by tempering flavors that are seen as volatile or exciting with a bowl of something that might at first appear bland. Within Cantonese cooking there is the concept of *qingdan* (清淡). These are light foods, not greasy or fried, but rather prized for their delicacy and restorative properties. They sit alongside roasted meats or soups made with pungent dried seafood. These are balancing acts that we in the West can appreciate, even if just from a flavor perspective.

This dish plays the part of gentle foil to richer dishes that might be consumed elsewhere in your diet. If you have an upset stomach in China, the first prescribed medicine will often be a cup of boiling hot water, which after the Communist Revolution became a mainstay of home medicine. Second to that will be a plainly flavored *zhou* (粥) or rice congee like this one. It's easy on the stomach, palate, and wallet.

10½ oz (300 g) pumpkin, peeled and cubed
1 cup (200 g) long-grain or jasmine rice, washed
3–4 dried jujube (red dates)
Granulated sugar, to taste
Youtiao (see page 77), to serve

Put the pumpkin into a pot or rice cooker and cover with water. Bring to a boil, or for the rice cooker use the "cook" or "steam" option, and cook until it is tender but not completely mushy.

Add the rice and dates to the pot or rice cooker and cover with water so that it is triple the depth of the rice.

Simmer the rice for 1 hour over medium heat, stirring occasionally so it doesn't stick to the bottom of the pot. Once cooked, the pumpkin will be very tender and the rice will be soft and starchy but still whole. Mash the pumpkin with a spoon and stir it into the rice. Top up with more water as needed to create your desired consistency.

Add sugar to your preference, although depending on how sweet your pumpkin was it might be none. Serve hot with the youtiao.

153

The Tianluokeng Tulou Cluster (nicknamed "four dishes and one soup"), a series of fortified villages still inhabited in rural Fujian province.

Rice and Other Grains

Chongqing You Cha

Chongqing Oil Tea
Serves 2

Other than the name of the city in the title, nothing is given away by the description of this dish. It has little to do with oil and nothing to do with tea. Instead, it's a very lazy way to make congee, using soaked rice that is ground to a mush and served as an easily digestible gruel. While gruel is such an unappetizing word, this is actually incredibly delicate and tasty. It is typically served in small bowls, much like the noodles of neighboring Sichuan province. Chongqing is now its own self-governing city, but some traditions make a lot of good sense.

I was fortunate to try one of the most delicious expressions of this dish one rainy morning when I was there. The only options I was given were whether I wanted it spicy and if I wanted cilantro. The smooth underbelly of rice is topped with crispy deep-fried wonton pieces, and the flavorings excite the senses and awaken you on dreary mornings without being a burden on the stomach.

The crispy topping can be prepared in advance, and it makes the most delicious snack. Don't be afraid to make a double or triple batch and store it in an airtight container lined with paper towels.

½ cup (100 g) glutinous rice
1 cup (250 ml) water
½ teaspoon finely chopped garlic
½ teaspoon finely chopped fresh root ginger
A pinch of MSG
½ teaspoon ground black pepper
A pinch of salt
2–3 teaspoons Chile Crisp (see page 282, or use store-bought)
1 tablespoon chopped roasted, unsalted peanuts
1–2 tablespoons chopped cilantro
1 teaspoon Sichuan pepper oil
2 oz (60 g) zhacai (pickled mustard greens), chopped
1¾ oz (50 g) deep-fried dumpling wrappers (see page 80, or use store-bought Indian sev)

Put the rice into a bowl, cover with water, and set aside to soak for at least 2 hours, or overnight.

Drain the rice and transfer it to a blender. Add the measured water and blend to a smooth paste.

Transfer the rice mixture to a saucepan and cook over medium-low heat, stirring constantly, until you have a thick, glossy porridge consistency. Add a little more water if necessary. Add the garlic, ginger, MSG, black pepper, and salt and stir well.

Divide between two small bowls and top with the chile crisp, peanuts, cilantro, Sichuan pepper oil, and zhacai. Add a generous handful of crushed fried wonton wrappers to finish.

Rice and Other Grains

Ci Fan Tuan

Shanghainese Filled Sticky Rice Rolls
Serves 2

What I love about this breakfast is its rather haphazard construction. A fistful of steamed rice is flattened into a disc, then an entire *youtiao* is rammed into the center of it. It is then topped with various pickles, pork floss, and sugar—and I like mine finished with a salted egg yolk. The entire thing is then pressed into a ball and popped in a bag. It's sort of the Shanghainese equivalent of a Scotch egg or empanada—a portable item that can take a lot of bashing but still remains intact in your bag or pocket.

My favorite place to buy this, on Wuding Lu in Shanghai, uses a mixture of black (but really purple) rice and regular white rice. During the breakfast rush there is no time to gently crumble in the egg, so it is just rammed in the middle, but that does mean each bite comes with a different flavor, and I absolutely love it. Some places use a bamboo mat like those used to roll sushi and the options are really as varied as your desires.

Once you've prepared the rice, the rest is just about preparing your mise en place. Then you can easily put together a breakfast that is filling, nutritious, and adaptable to your tastes and dietary needs.

1 cup (200 g) glutinous rice (all white or ½ cup/ 100 g black and ½ cup/100 g white)
1 Youtiao (see page 77), cut in half lengthways
2 tablespoons zhacai (pickled mustard greens)
2 tablespoons pickled radishes
2 salted duck egg yolks, crumbled
2 teaspoons granulated sugar
1¾ oz (50 g) pork floss

Put the rice into a bowl, cover with water, and set aside to soak for at least 2 hours.

Prepare a large steamer and line the basket with cheesecloth. Discard the soaking water and transfer the rice to the steamer, spreading it out to about ½ in (1 cm) thick, then cook for 20 minutes.

Lay a piece of plastic, cheesecloth, or a bamboo sushi mat on a plate. Take a generous handful of the hot rice and press it into a circle about the size of a saucer. Fold one of the halves of youtiao in half and cover it with a tablespoon each of the zhacai and pickled radishes. Crumble one of the salted duck egg yolks across and top with a teaspoon of sugar and half the pork floss, then wrap in the rice and smush it all into a ball. It should be the size of a large orange. Use some extra rice to patch up any holes so you have a tidy ball. Repeat with the remaining rice and fillings.

158

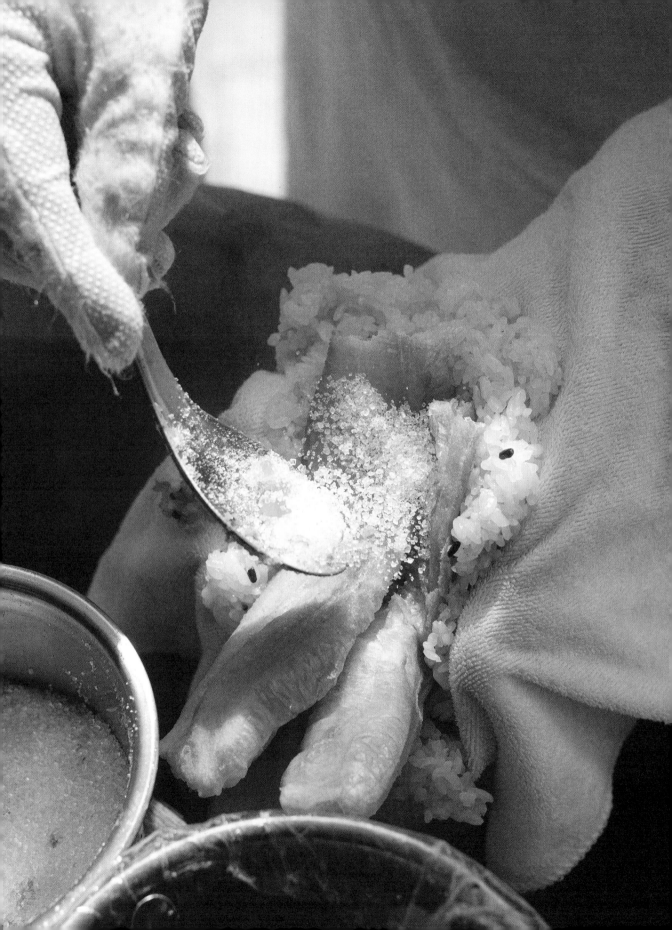

糯米银耳粥

Nuomi Yin Er Zhou

Sticky Eight-Treasure Rice with Snow Fungus
Serves 2

In the late 1990s, the city of Chongqing was separated from its mother province of Sichuan and became its own municipality of 30 million people. I've always found it interesting how arbitrary political divisions can lead to the evolution of a culinary landscape. New pathways are formed and, over time, distinctions grow.

While Chongqing cuisine is rooted in Sichuan, today I find that compared to Chengdu, Zigong, or Leshan, the food of Chongqing is more extreme, spicier, more sour, and has greater pungency. It takes a maximalist approach to flavor, with a greater focus on trend-driven commercialism, new restaurant openings, and products endorsed by KOLs ("key opinion leaders," China's name for social media influencers).

But still the classics remain, quiet and yet somehow brilliant. Eight-treasure rice is known across China in various forms. In Shanghai, it is a steamed rice cake. For Laba Festival in northern China it is usually served as a congee, but at one small restaurant I visited in Chongqing, it was served with *yin er* (银耳) fungus, also known as snow fungus (*Tremella fuciformis*), prized for its medicinal properties linked to anti-aging. With a delicate, sweet soup topped with ground black sesame seeds, it was certainly a departure from the regular spicy noodles of the region. I ordered the Chongqing You Cha (see page 156) as well and switched back and forth between sweet and spicy.

About ½ cup (80–100 g) short-grain or Arborio rice, washed
8 "treasures" of your choice—2 teaspoons each of any sort of nuts, mung beans, red beans, raisins, or any other dried fruit, dried coconut flakes, Job's tears, lotus seeds, dried jujube (red dates)
1 dried snow fungus
6⅓ cups (1.5 liters) water
3 oz (80 g) rock sugar
2 tablespoons ground black sesame seeds
1 teaspoon granulated sugar

161

Put the rice into a bowl with the treasures and cover everything with water, then set aside to soak for 2–3 hours.

Place the snow fungus in a bowl, cover it with water, and set aside to soak for 1 hour, or until soft. Once soft, remove the woody yellowish core and discard it. Cut the fungus into chunks and add to a pot with the measured water and rock sugar. Bring to a boil, then reduce to a simmer and cook for 40 minutes. You should have a light, sweet soup. Set aside and leave to cool slightly.

Meanwhile, stir together the ground black sesame seeds and sugar in a small bowl.

Drain the water from the rice and treasures and transfer them to a saucepan. Pour in enough water so that is it double the height of the rice. Bring to a boil, then when you see small holes starting to appear, reduce the heat to the lowest possible setting and cover tightly. Cook for a further 15 minutes, then remove from the heat and set aside to steam with the lid on for a further 15 minutes.

To serve, put a large scoop of the rice into a bowl, then pour a moat of the fungus soup around it and top with a tablespoon of black sesame and sugar.

Rice and Other Grains

Huangshan Cai Fan

Huangshan Vegetable Rice
Serves 2–3

黄山菜饭

In a corner of Laoximen, Shanghai, amidst the shadow of hyper-urban redevelopment, a single stretch of restaurants clings on. One of them, run by a husband and wife, makes Huangshan-style *cai fan* (菜饭), which can simply be translated as "vegetable rice." The owner tells all his customers that he is proudly from Huangshan, in Anhui province, and his recipe has never changed since he moved to Shanghai.

162

Scallion forms the flavor base for the dish, along with salt, chicken bouillon powder, and MSG. It is then topped with a fresh steamer full of rice and copious amounts of frozen, finely chopped *jicai* (荠菜), or shepherd's purse, which acts as a kind of green punctuation. It is added frozen so that it maintains its intense flavor and color. The whole thing is tossed with a customized shovel, like a sawn-off shotgun. I love how the Chinese ingeniously use hardware tools as cooking implements. I chatted with the couple as I waited for my food and they told me their days of operating are numbered. Not only because of gentrification in their neighborhood, but because they had no children to continue the business. Get your vegetable rice while it's still there.

The finished dish is served with a crispy fried egg and as much chile paste as you like. It is a simple, delicate, and very delicious breakfast. In the West you will most often find shepherd's purse in the freezer section of Asian supermarkets.

1 cup (200 g) long-grain rice
Scant 1 cup (200 ml) water
Scant ½ cup (100 ml) neutral oil
3–4 scallions, finely chopped
A pinch of salt
½ teaspoon chicken bouillon powder
A pinch of MSG
3½ oz (100 g) frozen chopped shepherd's purse

To serve
Fried eggs
Chile sauce of your choice

Put the rice into a bowl that will fit inside a steamer, then cover with water and set aside to soak for 1–2 hours.

Drain the rice, then wash it two or three times until the water runs a little clearer. Drain again and add back to the bowl with the measured water.

Prepare a steamer and steam the rice over medium heat for 20 minutes, then remove from the heat and set aside in the steamer for 5 minutes to continue cooking before removing the lid.

Heat the oil in a wok over high heat. Add the scallions, salt, chicken bouillon powder, and MSG and stir continuously for 2 minutes until the onion is softened.

Add the steamed rice and stir continuously until well incorporated and then add the frozen shepherd's purse. Stir through, then remove from the heat. You don't want to cook the shepherd's purse, just simply warm it through and preserve the fresh vibrant color and aroma.

Serve with the fried eggs and chile sauce.

艇仔粥

Ting Zai Zhou

Boat Congee

Serves 2

During the final days of China's zero-Covid policy, I decided to make a trip to Shunde in Guangdong province. What is so special about this small town on the outskirts of the megacity of Guangzhou is its legacy as a culinary center of Cantonese culture and cuisine. Usually bustling and electric, on my visit it was rather quiet and somber.

Walking the banyan tree-lined streets, I found that many of the restaurants were closed, but luckily I found a trio of ladies making good business from the lack of competition. With a row of 12 pans, they were turning out bowls of boat congee, also sometimes known as sampan congee. A sampan is a small, flat-bottomed fishing boat used by nomadic communities historically living on the sea of southern China. In Chinese they are now referred to as *shui shang ren* (水上人), or "on water people," but historically the Cantonese *tanka* was used to describe the communities of the Pearl River Delta. This is one of the few surviving recipes we can attribute to them. With the industrialization of the coastline over the last 200 years, many came to live on land and their culture and traditions have been lost. The shape of the pans the women were using was also interesting. They had a curved bottom that matched the shape of the ladle and meant they could get into the

corners effectively, addressing a design flaw many of us struggle with when cooking. A very satisfying design indeed.

The congee has a flavor base of pork and shrimp, with large pieces of carp and squid added at the end of the cooking. Purists would say that it's not really boat congee unless it's made and eaten on a boat.

¾ cup (150 g) short-grain rice, washed
5 cups (1.15 liters) water
¼ cup (30 g) raw peanuts, with skins
1¾ oz (50 g) fatty ground pork (15% fat)
5¼–7 oz (150–200 g) skinless white fish fillet, cut into thin slices
2 century eggs, peeled (optional)
1¾ oz (50 g) squid (rings and/or tentacles)
1¾ oz (50 g) peeled raw shrimp
1 thumb-sized piece of fresh root ginger, julienned
2 scallions, thinly sliced
Salt and white pepper
2 Youtiao (see page 77), sliced, to serve

Put the rice into a bowl, cover with ⅔ cups (150 ml) of the water and set aside to soak overnight.

Drain the water from the rice and discard. Put the rice into a pot and add the remaining 4⅓ cups (1 liter) of fresh water.

Cook over high heat for 10 minutes, stirring constantly, then reduce the heat to low and add the peanuts. Continue to cook, stirring frequently, for 30–40 minutes until the rice starts to soften and break down.

Add the pork, fish, and century eggs, if using. Mash the century eggs into the congee with a spoon and stir for 2–3 minutes. Add the squid and shrimp and when the shrimp turn pink the congee is ready to serve.

Check for seasoning, then add the ginger and scallions to finish. Serve with slices of youtiao.

165

Wuhan San Xian Dou Pi

武汉三鲜豆皮

Wuhan Three-Treasure Rice

Serves 4

There is something of a holy trinity of breakfast dishes in Wuhan (as there are in many places), made up of Re Gan Mian (see page 31), Mian Wo (see page 86), and this *san xian dou pi* (三鲜豆皮), although locally it is simply known as *dou pi* (豆皮).

An enormous crêpe is made with a mixture of rice and mung bean flour, then sealed with egg. Next, a mixture of sticky steamed rice is spread over the surface of the crêpe before a layer of pork, bamboo shoots, and mushrooms are added. These are the "three treasures" that give this dish its name, *san* (三) being the number three and *xian* (鲜) being treasure. In modern recipes, the pork is sometimes replaced with smoked tofu to make a vegetarian version.

The real excitement comes when the pan is grabbed and, with a flick of the wrist (and I'm sure a lot of core strength), the entire pancake is flipped over. A glug of brown spiced sauce is then poured around the edges. The excitement keeps going as the whole thing is divided up into pieces using the edge of a white plate. This is partly to protect the pan, which has developed years of patina and natural nonstick properties.

By the end, the serving is a large square, about 3 x 3 in (8 x 8 cm), with the three treasures on the bottom, rice in the middle, and a crispy glazed pancake covering on top. A few scallions dot the surface for prettiness and color.

Theoretically, you could make elements of this dish in advance, for example the pancake and the pork mixture. I would advise making something smaller than the street peddlers do in Wuhan, but if you're feeling lucky, bigger is always better.

→

Rice and Other Grains

Wuhan San Xian Dou Pi

1¼ cups (150 g) glutinous rice
9 oz (250 g) pork belly or 3½ oz (100 g) extra-firm
    smoked tofu, finely diced
3½ oz (100 g) chestnut mushrooms, finely diced
3½ oz (100 g) fresh bamboo shoots, blanched and
    finely diced (or canned bamboo shoots, rinsed)
3½ oz (100 g) extra-firm smoked tofu, finely diced
1 piece of cassia bark
1 bay leaf
1 star anise
1 tablespoon dark soy sauce
1 tablespoon light soy sauce
½–¾ oz (15–20 g) rock sugar, according to taste
2 scallions, chopped

For the pancake
½ cup (60 g) rice flour
½ cup (60 g) mung bean flour
¼ cup (30 g) cake flour
½ teaspoon fine salt
⅓ teaspoon ground white pepper
⅔ cups (150 ml) water
2 eggs
Neutral oil or lard, for frying and greasing

Put the glutinous rice into a bowl and cover with
water, then set aside to soak for at least 4 hours,
or ideally overnight.

For the pancake batter, combine the dry
ingredients in a bowl, then add the water and one
of the eggs. Whisk together, then set aside to
hydrate for 30 minutes.

Fry the pork belly in a dry frying pan (or the tofu
with a little oil) over medium heat for 8–10 minutes
until some of the fat has rendered out, then add
the mushrooms. They will act like little sponges
and soak up the flavor. Stir for a minute, then add
the rest of the ingredients, except the scallions.
Add a few tablespoons of water to create a sauce,
then cook for 5–7 minutes until the pork is fully
cooked and the rock sugar has dissolved. Remove
the cassia bark, bay leaf, and star anise and set
aside to cool.

Prepare a large steamer and line the basket
with cheesecloth. Discard the soaking water
and transfer the rice to the steamer, then cook
over medium-high heat for 15 minutes. Remove
from the heat but leave the lid on. This will create

further stickiness so that the rice adheres to
the pancake.

Heat a little oil or lard in a flat-bottomed frying
pan over medium heat, then add enough batter
to create a thin layer. After 2 minutes, whisk the
remaining egg and pour it over the pancake, using
a spatula to ensure even coverage.

When the egg is nearly fully cooked, flip the
pancake over. Pour a little more oil or lard around
the edge so that the pancake browns. Remove the
pan from the heat.

If you have asbestos hands, take the hot rice
and press it onto the pancake in the pan in a ½ in
(1–1.5 cm) thick layer. Otherwise, use gloves or a
flexible spatula.

Add a layer of the three-treasure mixture (minus
the cooking liquid) and press it into the rice.

Smear a little oil on a plate and place it over the
pan, then flip it onto the plate. Slide the assembled
pancake back into the pan and place back over
medium heat.

Pour some of the three-treasure cooking liquid
around the edge of the pancake and cook for
3–4 minutes just to bring the temperature of the
cooking liquid up.

Slide the pancake onto a large serving plate and
cut into quarters. Sprinkle over the scallions
before serving.

Lawei Nuomi Fan

Sticky Rice with Preserved Vegetables, Dried Shrimp, and Pork

Serves 4

腊味糯米饭

What I like so much about this dish is that it feels like a casual version of *lo mai gai* (糯米 雞), the glutinous rice parcel steamed in lotus leaves that, to me, is an essential part of any dim sum breakfast.

Here, the flavorings are less complicated and the process less technical, too. As a simple breakfast eaten on the streets of Guangzhou, it also felt like a distant experience from the formality of a sit-down dim sum meal with family. I had a generous portion rammed into a small plastic bowl that was deceptively heavy. The rice wasn't fused

together into a rice cake texture like a *zongzi* (粽子), the glorious pyramid-shaped rice parcels popular during Dragon Boat Festival, but it was still compact enough that eating it with chopsticks was no problem.

Soak the rice overnight and then you will have a delicious breakfast very quickly the next morning. While the side of eggs was not on the menu when I first tried this, I always serve it with them when I make it at home. To make this vegan, you could remove the pork belly, sausage, and dried shrimp and replace them with firm smoked tofu.

Lawei Nuomi Fan

For the rice
2⅔ cups (500 g) glutinous rice
1 tablespoon dark soy sauce
2 teaspoons light soy sauce
½ teaspoon salt
½ teaspoon ground white pepper
Lotus leaves, soaked, for steaming (optional)

For the toppings
1 tablespoon dark soy sauce
2 teaspoons light soy sauce
2 tablespoons Shaoxing wine
1 teaspoon granulated sugar
½ teaspoon ground white pepper
3½ oz (100 g) pork belly, cubed or thinly sliced
    (optional)
2 lap cheong (Cantonese-style dried sausage),
    thinly sliced
1¾ oz (50 g) dried shrimp, soaked
1¾ oz (50 g) wood ear mushrooms, soaked
    and chopped
⅓ cup (50 g) raw peanuts, with skins
3 scallions, finely chopped
Fried eggs, to serve (optional)

172

Put the rice into a bowl and cover with water, then leave to soak for a minimum of 6 hours, or overnight.

To prepare the toppings, combine the dark and light soy sauce, Shaoxing wine, sugar, and white pepper in a bowl, then add the pork belly and set aside to marinate for 30–60 minutes.

Drain the rice and transfer it to a bowl, then add the dark and light soy sauce, salt, and white pepper and mix until evenly distributed.

Prepare a steamer and line the basket either with the lotus leaves or with parchment paper. If using parchment paper, poke or cut plenty of holes in it.

Add a layer of the rice to the steamer, followed by some of the pork, sausage, shrimp, mushrooms, peanuts, and scallion. Repeat this layering until you run out of rice, finishing with a layer of toppings for aesthetic appeal.

Cover loosely with more lotus leaves or a piece of parchment paper with holes poked in it and steam over high heat for 20–25 minutes until the rice and pork belly are cooked.

Remove from the heat, but leave the steamer covered for 5 minutes. This will help to enhance the sticky texture of the rice.

Using a rice paddle or large spoon, give the rice a mix to break it up before serving.

Xian Nai Mi Bu

Kunming Rice Pudding
Serves 1

鮮奶米布

There is something deeply comforting about a bowl of *mi bu* (米布), a silky rice cream of sorts found in Kunming, the provincial capital of Yunnan.

The first time I tried it, something in my memory was stirred. It was new, yet completely familiar, like porridge and rice pudding combined. In appearance it might look like PVA glue, but its velvet-smooth texture and delicate sweetness is delicious on its own, or it can act as a canvas to other, more dynamic flavors.

On my most recent visit to Kunming, I asked if I could go into the kitchen to see how it was made. Stacks of small clay pots are prepared in advance, with a bit of water, some white sugar, and two scoops of finely ground *xiaomi* (小米), a type of small-grained rice not to be confused with millet, even though it has the same name and characters. When the orders come in, the pot is put on an enormous flame and stirred vigorously with chopsticks. Then a squirt of fresh milk goes in and that's it.

For some time not much happens, but suddenly after a few minutes of stirring, the rice starch begins to gelatinize, and it thickens in seconds. As it comes away from the sides of the pot, the heat is turned off and the stirring continues.

I prefer it absolutely unadulterated, but I did witness other customers adding a scant drizzle of soy sauce and chile crisp.

3 tablespoons rice flour
3½ tablespoons whole milk
1 tablespoon granulated sugar
⅓ cup (75 ml) water

Put all the ingredients into a small clay pot over high heat and use a pair of long cooking chopsticks to stir until well combined.

Cook undisturbed for 2–3 minutes. Nothing much will happen at first, but when the heat picks up, start stirring continuously. After 7–8 minutes you will feel the mixture start to thicken. This is when you need to pick up the pace and stir quickly until it comes together into a smooth consistency.

Remove the pudding from the heat and keep stirring for a further 30 seconds.

Slide the clay pot onto a plate and serve.

175

Xibo Zao Fan
Xibonese Breakfast

In the village of Qapqal Xibe, in western Xinjiang, I had breakfast in a charming restaurant where the courtyard was painted hot Barbie pink. My friend Atina had told her family I was coming; a foreigner with an interest in what was on the menu for breakfast. There was a small crowd gathered to see me, and I was introduced to the family, neighbors, and a few children who had never seen a foreigner in real life.

A table was set up in the courtyard with a linen tablecloth and a procession of small plates arrived from the kitchen. Pickled radishes with chile, *pao cai* (泡菜), which most would recognize as a white kimchi, roasted red peppers with garlic chives, carrot salads, roasted green peppers with eggplant, soy-pickled garlic with sugar, and a finely chopped spicy red pepper with scallions. Some of these dishes would be difficult to replicate in other parts of China, let alone in other far-flung corners of the world.

The origins of the Xibonese people are rooted in Jilin province, in the northeast part of China bordering North Korea. While it is often a hot topic to discuss and trace the various paths of Chinese external migration over the centuries (including that of my own family story), internal migration is rarely considered, whether that movement is due to displacement or economic reasons. In a country as big as China, moving across a vast distance to the other side of the nation can feel as alien as relocating to a foreign country.

During the Qing Dynasty, the Xibo were considered one of the eight elite forces of the military. In 1764, 18,000 of them were relocated to Xinjiang—a 2,175 mile (3,500 km) journey under escort—dividing their culture into two. Used to suppress revolutions and expand the Chinese frontier (Xinjiang literally translates as "new frontier"), the Xibo also served a double purpose under a *tuntian* (屯田) system. These were military-run farms that turned harsh landscapes into agrarian settler colonies. In the last 250 years, the Xibo in Xinjiang have preserved their language and religion, a blend of shamanism and Buddhism. Today, the Xibo people are split across opposite sides of the country, with around 100,000 of them in Xinjiang and another 200,000 in Jilin.

The majority of the Xibonese menu is comprised of a selection of cold vegetables, fermented and pickled roots, and salads. Other dishes demonstrate the influence of their arrival in Xinjiang, the incoming cuisine acting as a kind of culinary sponge. These include a fluffy flatbread that is reminiscent of *laffa* from the Islamic tradition, leavened with sourdough starter, baking powder, and baking soda; delicate fruit compotes, an influence from Russia and Kazakhstan; and a dish of dried milk skin called *urum*, thicker than that used in the Xibo salty milk tea (see page 178), which is a common thread shared among the cultures of the Silk Road, from Turkey to Mongolia.

Nai Zi Pi and Nai Cha

Milk Skin and Salty Milk Tea
Serves 4–5

Since the rest of world practically chugs tea and coffee for breakfast, it might seem surprising that the Chinese are not usually so caffeinated in the mornings.

With the exception of Guangdong in the south and some areas of Fujian, the only other area of China that consumes tea in the early morning is Xinjiang. From Uyghurs to Kazakhs to Xibonese, a large bowl of salty milk tea is a must for any breakfast table. Served as part of the full Xibonese breakfast experience or simply with a few Kazakh Baursak (see page 85), this drink is actually more about the milk than the tea.

I visited the aunt of a friend who runs a small side hustle in Xinjiang making milk skin for a special restaurant in Shanghai. Fatty, rich, unpasteurized, and unhomogenized milk is slowly heated over charcoal in the outdoor kitchen. The process splits the milk into two products. One is a fatty and rich skin and the other is a lighter milk that forms the main body of the salty tea.

The tea itself might take some getting used to; its saltiness is not to everyone's taste. I would recommend starting with a half teaspoon of sugar and a large pinch of salt and adjusting to your preference.

Generous 2 cups (500 ml) raw, unpasteurized, unhomogenized whole milk
Sea salt
Granulated sugar (optional)
Strong black tea, freshly brewed

Preheat the oven to the lowest setting, usually around 230°F (110°C), selecting the lower element function (so that it only heats from the bottom).

Pour the milk into a large frying pan over medium heat. Gently heat the milk for 12–15 minutes until a fine skin starts to form. At no point during this process do you want the milk to bubble or boil. Be prepared to turn the heat down and watch it like a hawk, as milk can overflow in a jiffy.

Once the skin has formed, whisk the milk continuously for 15 minutes. You want a nice foamy texture. Next, reduce the heat to low and continue to whisk for a further 10 minutes. You might need to change arms or find an assistant.

You now need to leave the milk to cook very gently and form its skin. The best way to replicate the continuous low heat of coals in a Western home kitchen is to use the oven. Place the pan directly onto the bottom of the oven and leave to cook, uncovered, for 1 hour, leaving the oven door open.

After 1 hour, turn off the oven and leave the milk to cool to body temperature.

To prepare the tea, put a pinch of salt and sugar, if using, into a cereal bowl.

Using a spoon, scrape off some ragged pieces of the milk skin and add them to the bowl. Ladle a few spoonfuls of milk over the skin and top it with an equal quantity of tea.

If you want a stronger brew, it's important to remember that a longer infusion time doesn't give more strength or flavor, just bitterness. To make a stronger tea, use more tea!

Top with a dash of boiling water to your liking.

The milk skin can be frozen for 2–3 months, or, if you have a food dehydrator, it can be dried at 140°F (60°C) for 6–8 hours.

奶子皮

奶茶

A mosque undergoes renovation in a village near Shanshan, Xinjiang.

Xibonese Breakfast

锡伯饼子

Xibo Bingzi

Xibonese Bread
Makes 4 breads

At the center of the Xibonese breakfast spread is a large, soft, and fluffy bread that is cooked in a frying pan with just a tiny amount of oil.

The hydration (water to flour ratio) here is very high. As such, it has great elasticity, handling similarly to pizza dough. In the restaurant at Qapqal Xibe, they used a sourdough starter to make theirs, adding extra baking powder and baking soda to produce a bread of incredible lightness.

If you are using a sourdough starter at home, work out 20 percent of the weight of the flour and use that amount of starter—so in this case, 3 oz (80 g). All sourdough starters behave differently, however, and you will know yours better than me. For sourdough *bingzi*, leave the dough to rise overnight at room temperature. Otherwise, using instant yeast and proofing in the fridge will achieve similar results.

One important point to note is that the Xibo do not salt their bread, instead relying on the salted and pickled vegetables served with it to provide seasoning.

3⅓ cups (400 g) all-purpose flour,
    plus extra for dusting
1 tablespoon instant yeast
1½ cups (350 ml) water
2 teaspoons baking powder
½ teaspoon baking soda
1 tablespoon neutral oil

Put half the flour, the yeast, and the water into a bowl and give it a good stir. Cover and transfer to the fridge. Leave to rise overnight until you have a bubbly and fragrant liquid batter.

The next day, remove the bowl from the fridge and allow to come to room temperature for 1 hour. Add the baking powder and baking soda and enough of the remaining flour to create a soft and elastic dough, similar to pizza dough. You might not need all of it, so add it ½ cup (60 g) at a time.

Tip the dough out onto a lightly floured surface, weigh it, then divide it into four equal-sized portions.

Press each piece out into a circle the size of the frying pan you will use. You want each piece to be roughly ¾–1 in (2–3 cm) thick.

Brush the frying pan with a little of the oil and place over low heat.

Add one of the breads to the pan and fry for 10–12 minutes until the bottom develops a light golden brown crust and large bubbles start to form on top. Flip the bread over and cook for a further 10–12 minutes. Repeat with the remaining dough.

If the breads are still raw in the middle after this time, wrap them in foil, and bake them in the oven at 350°F (180°C) for 10–15 minutes.

Xibo Zu Hua Hua Cai

Xibonese Slaw
Serves 6–8

One of the essential cold dishes of a
Xibonese breakfast. Essentially, it's a slaw,
which is salted and chilled for two days
before being served with bread.

This is heavily salted as it is usually eaten
with unsalted bread (see page 183). If you
prefer, you can use less, so I have offered a
range in the recipe below that you can adjust
according to your taste.

1 lotus root
3–4 carrots
⅓ daikon
3 green peppers
3 red peppers
3½ oz (100 g) garlic chives
3–6 tablespoons kosher or coarse sea salt

Shred or julienne all the vegetables to the same
size and thickness—a long matchstick is perfect.

Put all the vegetables into a large container and
add the salt. Mix thoroughly so that the salt is
evenly distributed.

Cover and chill in the fridge for 2 days.

When you're ready to serve, take it out of the
fridge an hour before so that is chilled but not
fridge-cold.

184

Jiucai Lajiang

Garlic Chive and Red Pepper Salad

Serves 3–4

This is really more of a relish than a salad. The pepper used here is a cousin of the Turkish Urfa biber. It is longer than a regular red pepper, with a pointed end. This dish is on the very mildest end of spicy, with a rounded sweetness and a touch of smoke.

There are plenty of ways to add a smoky taste, such as smoked salt, liquid smoke, or by grilling your peppers over charcoal or an open flame. I like to add some Turkish pul biber to give it extra body and dimension.

2 Turkish red peppers (or roasted red peppers in oil)
1–2 teaspoons pul biber (Aleppo pepper flakes)
5½ oz (150 g) garlic chives, finely chopped
A pinch of salt

Char the peppers over a flame until blackened or roast them in the oven at 425°F (220°C) until soft.

Place the hot peppers in a plastic bag, a bowl covered with plastic wrap, or a plastic container, and set aside to steam for 10 minutes.

Peel the skins from the peppers, remove the seeds, and discard both.

Finely dice the peppers, then combine them with the rest of the ingredients in a bowl. Stir thoroughly, then set aside let the flavors mingle for 1 hour before serving.

Xibonese Breakfast

Doufu
Soy and Tofu

The character *dou* (豆) in Mandarin Chinese can be used to describe an entire universe of beans, from mung beans (*lu dou*, 绿豆) and red beans (*hong dou*, 红豆) to peas (*wan dou*, 豌豆). But, as a character alone, it simply refers to the king of them all: the soy bean. Soy is one of the five ancient crops of Chinese civilization, known in this context as *wugu* (五谷). The others are millet (*su*, 粟), sesame (*ma*, 麻), barley (*mai*, 麦), and rice (*dao*, 稻). You will notice that these ancient classifiers differ from the modern characters used for rice, soy, millet and so on today.

Soy proteins are difficult to digest, but the ancient Chinese discovered that fermentation, sprouting, and grinding increased both nutritional value and flavor. Soy milk is the first process in the beans' journey to tofutopia, and for breakfast it is served either with a spoonful of white sugar or poured over vinegar and other salty condiments so that it curdles into a complex medley. The different regions of China are split on which is the best way to prepare it, usually with disdain for the other, but I didn't grow up drinking soy milk for breakfast and as an adult I enjoy both options equally.

Soy has been long recognized by the Chinese as an important crop during famine, as it fixes the nitrogen in the soil, removing the need for a fallow year. Its waste can be used as a rich fertilizer and its oil is used for cooking, as an engineering lubricant and in lighting. However, it wasn't until the twentieth century that the rest of the world took notice. Today, the largest grower of soy is the United States, with China way down the list in terms of annual production.

Two of the other key soy products, soy bean paste and soy sauce, have over two thousand years of history behind them, with experimentation and innovation starting from a single bean. The beans are taken through a process of aerobic growth and then anaerobic digestion in order to produce a salty liquid or paste that is a cornerstone of cooking for most of Asia. Tofu evolved almost a thousand years later. This process of making soy curds, both smooth and creamy but also textural and grainy, is nothing short of genius. The technique and terminology run almost parallel to cheese production. These curds can be dried, pressed, and manipulated into countless varieties and preparations, from skins, sticks, puffs, and smoked. And it doesn't end there. With fermented, hairy and stinky varieties, there is a tofu for absolutely everyone's preference (when it comes to fermented tofu, called *furu* 腐乳, I am absolutely evangelical).

In the last few years, tofu has found a new fan base in the West as a "meat substitute," but this is still only part of its immense flexibility. The different sweet, salty, or spicy combinations with tofu are almost infinite, and it can be a vehicle for flavor both as a supporting act or leading role. I hope that through a journey into China our understanding of soy and tofu can be expanded.

Doujiang 豆浆

Soy Milk
Serves 3–4

Whether you are from northern or southern China will determine the way that you are introduced to, raised on, and prefer your soy milk.

In the south, the soy milk is served sweet, with just a few teaspoons of sugar and nothing else. On the side you might have a *youtiao* or another breakfast pastry for dipping. In the north, the milk is served with a savory twist (see page 192).

Making fresh soy milk is no big deal. It's as basic as making a cup of tea or coffee. Why would a cookbook need a recipe for how to make a cup of tea? Because people make tea wrong all the time. Well, perhaps not wrong, but at least not in a way that pays respect to the product.

Once you know how to make soy milk, you will realize that not only is it superior to anything you can get in a carton, but that it can be the starting point for you to explore an entire world of tofu and tofu recipes.

½ cup (100 g) dried soy beans
4⅔ cups (1.1 liters) water
Granulated sugar, to serve (optional)

Put the soy beans in a bowl, cover with water, and set aside to soak for a minimum of 8 hours, or overnight. They are ready when they are plump and soft enough to break between your fingers.

Drain the beans and transfer them to a blender, then add the measured water and blend until smooth.

Pour the mixture into a large pot and bring to a gentle simmer. Cook for 15 minutes, stirring constantly and adjusting the heat if it looks like it's going to boil over. This process extracts as much of the bean flavor as possible while also neutralising any raw flavors that would make it unpleasant.

Remove from the heat and allow to cool slightly.

Place a fine sieve over a bowl and use a ladle to pour the thick milk through to remove most of the mash. You will need to scrape out the bean mash otherwise it will clog the sieve.

Place a piece of cheesecloth in the sieve, then repeat this filtering process once more. Finally, bundle up the cloth and give it a squeeze to extract as much liquid as possible. (In Beijing, the leftover bean mash is left out to dry for a day and then fried with lamb fat as a filling side dish to have with hot pot. You can also use it to bulk out things like veggie burgers, smoothies, or to thicken soups. It is full of fiber so don't just throw it out!)

Once the milk has been filtered, return it to the pot and bring it to a boil, then boil for 3–4 minutes.

Serve in the desired way, savory like a northerner (see page 192) or with a little sugar, like a southerner.

190

Xian Doujiang

Savory Soy Milk
Serves 3–4

While *xian* (咸) translates literally as "salty," I would describe this dish as "savory" soy milk instead. For the uninitiated, it sounds much more approachable, and there is much more going on here than just salt.

A bowl is preloaded with a few teaspoons of black vinegar, scallion, and a pinch of dried shrimp, then scalding-hot soy milk is poured on top. The vinegar triggers a curdling reaction that is highly prized. The texture is somewhat like a delicate custard. It's finished with a drizzle of chile oil and a few chunks of *youtiao*, which become soft and mushy, like a cookie dunked into a cup of tea.

Prepare the fresh soy milk following the instructions on page 190, then with a few extra store pantry ingredients you can transform that simple milk into an extraordinarily delicious breakfast. If you don't use the dried shrimp then this recipe is vegan, too.

1 x quantity Soy Milk (see page 190)
1 teaspoon dried shrimp
2 tablespoons Zhenjiang vinegar
1 tablespoon light soy sauce
1 tablespoon zhacai (pickled mustard greens) or other Chinese pickles of your choice
1 teaspoon sesame oil (optional)
1 x quantity Doujiang, hot (see page 190)
1 scallion (green part only), thinly sliced
½ Youtiao (see page 77), cut into pieces
Chile oil, to serve

First, toast the dried shrimp in a dry, nonstick frying pan over low-medium heat. This brings out their fragrance considerably.

Combine the shrimp, vinegar, soy sauce, zhacai, and sesame oil, if using, in a bowl.

Ladle over the hot soy milk—it must be hot, otherwise you won't get the desired effect. Leave to curdle for 30–40 seconds.

Garnish with the scallion, youtiao, and chile oil, then dig in.

Douhua 豆花

Tofu Pudding
Serves 4–6

In the countryside of Sichuan, a woman stands over a wok embedded into the counter that is filled with freshly made soy milk. She holds a large, crystal-like rock of gypsum and gently submerges it. Within seconds, the milk begins to curdle. Her spell is like that of a soy mage—or maybe she is a tofu witch. This ancient, gentle alkalizing process made some of the most delicious *douhua* (豆花) I have ever tried. It was textural and gritty, paired with spicy cold dishes and white rice.

If you've mastered the basics of making soy milk, the next logical step is to try making douhua. Literally translated as "soy bean flower," douhua is to the Chinese what *fior di latte* (milk flower) is to the Italians. The "flowering" blossom of the soy bean is complex, off-white, and a little jiggly. Its soft yet firm texture is like just-set pudding, cool and creamy. It is also a multidirectional blank canvas. It can be hot or cold, sweet or savory, ultra-smooth and pudding-like or with the textural grittiness of some yogurts. I prefer the latter consistency. It is a sort of halfway between the milk and tofu we would recognize in the West, a delicate and deliciously flexible thing in its own right.

Heating the milk first helps to denature the proteins and prepares them for the next step. A coagulant is then used, traditionally gypsum, or *shigao* (石膏). I have tried alternatives such as agar agar, citric acid, and nigari, but I really don't see the need for alternatives. Not only is gypsum safe (and has been used for hundreds of years), but it is also suitable for everyone including vegans and, most importantly of all, it gives the most reliable results. For the volume of douhua we want to make at home, gypsum is enough.

This recipe tries to replicate what I had in the village of Yuantong in Sichuan, which was like cottage cheese or even fresh ricotta. The soy whey that separates can be spooned over white rice for a delicious secondary dish.

Gypsum is available at most large Asian supermarkets and, of course, online. You can even buy gypsum stones on eBay and have a fabulous new kitchen prop. Other than the gypsum, this recipe requires no specialist equipment; however, a wok works best.

→

195

Soy and Tofu

Douhua

8½ cups (2 liters) fresh, homemade soy milk
   (double the recipe on page 190)
¼ oz (7 oz) gypsum, or a piece of gypsum stone

Optional toppings and sides
Cooked white rice
Spicy cold pickles
Cooked green vegetables
Eggs (fried, boiled or century eggs)
Fermented tofu (I like the spicy variety
   from Yunnan)

Pour the soy milk into a wok over medium-high
heat and gently warm it until it starts to steam.
Do not let it simmer or boil.

Put a few teaspoons of the hot milk into a bowl
and stir in the gypsum. Add this back to the milk
and gently stir with a ladle. If you are using a piece
of gypsum stone, carefully submerge the rock in
the milk and stir.

After 8–10 minutes, soft curds will start to form.
Reduce the heat to low and leave to cook gently
for a further 10 minutes without disturbing it.

Boil a kettle and, using the ladle, gently spoon a
thin layer of boiling water on top so that there is
less of a heat discrepancy between the top and
bottom of the pan.

Once you have a firm mass, use a knife (something
like a long bread knife without a sharp tip is ideal) to
cut the tofu into squares about 2 x 2 in (5 x 5 cm).

The fresh douhua is now ready to eat as you
wish. Any leftovers can be pressed into whatever
density of tofu you prefer. Wrap the curds in some
cheesecloth and place in a colander. Press the
tofu with a pan filled with some heavy cans and
leave it overnight. This makes a great homestyle
firm tofu that can be sliced, fried, crumbled, or
even smoked.

197

Sanzi Douhua

Savory Tofu Pudding with a Twist
Serves 3–4

嚻子豆花

198

This *douhua* (豆花) dish from Chengdu is something of an amalgamation of influences from the region. It combines a spicy meat sauce very similar to that used for Dan Dan Mian (see page 36) with crispy noodles called *sanzi* (嚻子) and chilled, freshly made douhua, all finished with a few spoonfuls of chile oil to ramp up the heat. The finished dish is a wonderful contrast of textures and temperatures and is one of my personal favorite ways to eat douhua.

1 x quantity Douhua (see page 195)
1 x quantity meat sauce from Dan Dan Mian (see page 36)
1 x quantity crispy deep-fried noodles from Chongqing You Cha (see page 156)

To serve
Chile Crisp (see page 282, or use store-bought) or chile oil
Roasted, unsalted peanuts, chopped
Scallions (green part only), thinly sliced
Cilantro leaves

Preparing this dish is just a matter of assembling the layers.

Half-fill a bowl with douhua and top it with a few spoonfuls of the dan dan sauce, a generous handful of crispy noodles, and some chile crisp or chile oil.

Garnish with the chopped peanuts, scallion, and cilantro.

The twist
At a small restaurant on Xi Da Jie in Chengdu, you also have the option to top a regular portion of dan dan noodles with douhua. It might seem like a lot, but only a child given a choice would pick just one. Douhua, noodles, meat sauce, and crunchy noodle bits… there are moments in life where such decisions are necessary and also very good.

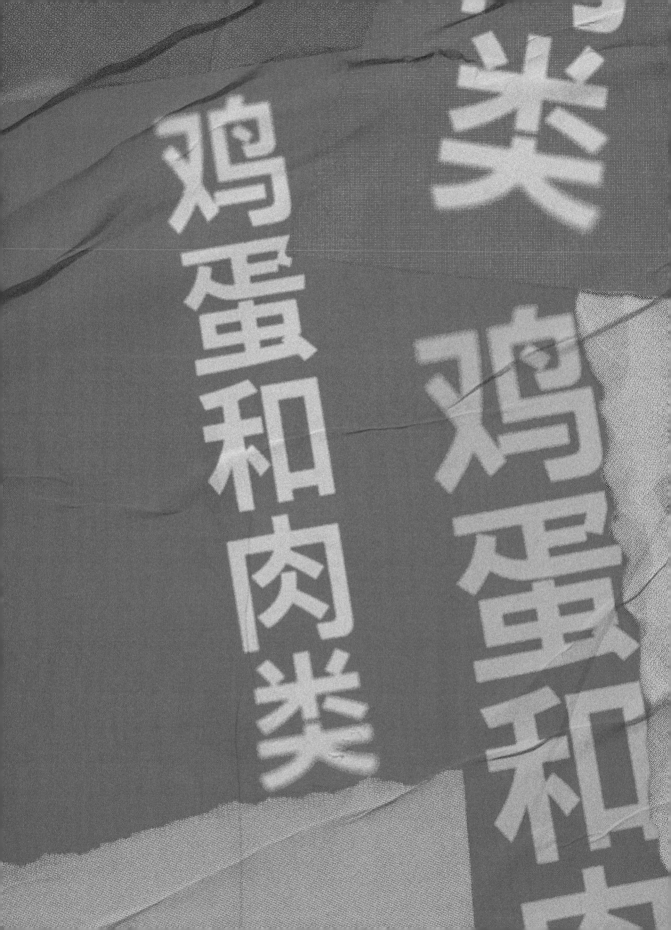

Jidan He Roulei
Eggs and Some Meat

If you look closely at the character for meat, *rou* (肉), you can see that it looks like the ribcage of an animal hung up for slaughter. The meaning of meat in Chinese society is manifested in many other ways too, from the spiritual to its economic symbolism. In Taiwan's national museum is the *rouxingshi* (肉形石), a Qing Dynasty sculpture cut from solid jasper to resemble a deliciously realistic piece of *dong po* pork. Its companion object is a piece of translucent jade cut to resemble a cabbage. It is the museum's most popular object and regularly goes on international tour. I even have the fridge magnet version at home.

At one end of the spectrum, meat represents wealth and prosperity. To have meat on the table is a signifier of success or a prosperous life. China lacks quality pastureland for large farm animals and so beef, and therefore also dairy, are largely missing. Smaller animals like pigs, ducks, and chickens that graze the land or live off scraps are the dominant animal protein even today.

When I first started to visit China as a young man, I was the guest of honor at family gatherings—one of the grandsons of Pao San had returned to the motherland! No extravagance was spared and, to commemorate this moment of joy, the table at dinner was laden with retro dishes and meats, including dong po pork, tea-smoked pigeons, velveteen beef, sweet and sour squirrel fish, and even Shanghainese-style snake.

At the other end of the spectrum, there is a philosophy that meat is simply unnecessary. This idea is influenced by Buddhism, further molded by a love of soy and tofu and cemented by ancient prejudices against foreigners and Western capitalism. My dearest Auntie Lizhu follows a lay Buddhist diet and only indulges in meat on set days of the year.

Across the recipes of this book, I wouldn't say meat plays an enormously important role at the breakfast table. You won't find yourself serving sausages or bacon like you would in the UK or US. That's not to say animal products aren't important, with lard being a key pillar of flavor and frugality, but they are generally not essential if you want to remove them. Even in Shanghai, modern food tech substitutes for eggs and meat are now available alongside the more traditional Chinese options for those who want to veganize their *jianbing*.

Eggs serve a greater role as a viable source of protein, but it's important to remember that even eggs are seasonal. Spring is a period of renewal and plenty, with the rest of the year focusing on century eggs as a prized delicacy. Try stirring century eggs into your breakfast congee for a decadent garnish or enjoy them how some young Chinese do, by muddling them into coffee.

Wuxiang Chaye Dan

五香茶叶蛋

Five-Flavor Tea Eggs
Makes 6 eggs

Spiced tea eggs are a god-tier Chinese breakfast food. They exemplify quite clearly the ability of Chinese cuisines to take inexpensive and accessible everyday ingredients and transform them into delicious things. I remember vividly a chain shop of Baba Mantou in Shanghai that would have a cauldron of tea eggs simmering away on the street edge, which I would pass by on my way to the metro. Often, customers would snack on them as they waited for a fresh batch of *baozi* to come out. Across the road is a 7Eleven where you could pick up a tea egg for as little as 2RMB (30 cents).

My only issue with tea eggs bought on the street is their sometimes peculiar texture, ranging from unctuous to rubber. For the sake of economy and nostalgia they're worth the experience, but if you want something more to your liking then nothing beats making them at home. Typically, if you are making a batch of a dozen eggs or more, then using a rice cooker is best, as many of them have a "keep warm" function that gently sous vides the eggs over many hours. Steeping them in the spice mix overnight will achieve a similar result.

These eggs are great for smaller appetites that want just a little fragrant protein hit. They're infinitely customizable, too—make them as pungent and spiced as you like, or go off-piste like I did, switching out the ancient tea for contemporary coffee from Yunnan (see page 204). If you want to use a rice cooker for this recipe, double the ingredients.

6 eggs
2 star anise
2 bay leaves
1 piece of cassia bark or 1 cinnamon stick
2 teaspoons cumin seeds
2½ tablespoons granulated sugar
1 tablespoon salt
4–5 tablespoons dark soy sauce
6–7 tablespoons light soy sauce
Generous 2 cups (500 ml) water
2½ teaspoons loose-leaf black tea

First, soft-boil the eggs. My preferred method is to start them in a pot of cold water and bring it to a boil, then simmer for 1 minute before removing them from the heat and setting aside in the pot for 5–6 minutes. Remove the eggs and transfer them to a bowl of iced water to chill for 8–10 minutes.

Once chilled, use the back of a teaspoon to gently crack the shells all over the surface of the eggs.

Put all the other ingredients into a pot and bring to a gentle simmer for 5 minutes. Add the eggs and simmer on the lowest heat for 1 hour. If you're using a rice cooker, use the "cook" function first to bring the marinade to a boil and then add the eggs, switching the setting to the "warm" function for 1 hour.

After 1 hour, remove the pot from the heat and leave to cool slightly. Transfer the eggs and the marinade to a container with a lid and set aside at room temperature to further marinate for at least 8 hours, or overnight.

To serve, peel and either eat as a snack or add it to a bowl of your favorite noodles. These will keep for 2 days in the fridge.

Kafei
Dan

咖啡蛋

Coffee Eggs
Makes 6 eggs

For those of you who have had the pleasure of eating a breakfast in China, you'll be familiar with the tea eggs on page 202. This recipe is my own invention, reflecting the emerging coffee culture in China. Domestic consumption is exploding in a country that is traditionally a tea-drinking nation. Shanghai now has more coffee shops per person than any city in the world and the trickle-down effect into smaller towns and cities is happening at a rapid pace.

I feel that recipes are a mirror of the time and place they were created, and there is no good reason why recipes cannot evolve with the times. Taking inspiration from the way Japanese ramen eggs are made, I decided to forego the cracking of the shells and peel them off entirely. I believe flavor wins over beauty any day.

Yunnan coffee is now readily available around the world, but if you can't find it then the nearest in flavor would be a single-origin Ethiopian coffee—something acidic and fruity.

⅔ cup (50 g) ground Yunnan coffee
1 cup (250 ml) light soy sauce
4¼ cups (1 liter) water
1 cinnamon stick
2 star anise
6 black peppercorns
1 teaspoon granulated sugar
1 teaspoon salt
A glug of Shaoxing wine or dry sherry
2 teaspoons Sichuan peppercorns
6 eggs

Combine all the ingredients in a pot, except the eggs.

Bring to a gentle boil, then simmer for 5 minutes. Remove from the heat and leave to cool, then transfer to a lidded container. This stage can be done in advance.

Put the eggs into a pot and fill with tepid water. Bring to a boil, then simmer for 1 minute before removing them from the heat and setting aside in the pot for 6½ minutes. Remove the eggs and transfer them to a bowl of iced water to chill.

Peel the eggs, then add them to the cooled coffee mixture. Chill in the fridge for 24 hours.

When you're ready to eat, remove the eggs from the marinade (you could save this for another batch).

Hai Li Jian

Oyster Omelet
Serves 2

All along the coast of Fujian province you will find some expression of an oyster and egg dish. Most of the time it will be a formal half-moon shaped omelet concealing a jiggly mass of translucent and sweet oysters, but sometimes, like this one, it will be a hurried looking hash of a scramble.

I was in the town of Shishi (in Mandarin, the word for "city" is also *shi*, so this is a great tongue twister: *shi shi shi*), not far from Quanzhou, and in what appeared to be the entrance to an underground parking lot was a restaurant specializing in fried oysters. These tiny oysters are no larger than a grape and they were all shucked by hand. First the oysters were added to a pan, then eggs were scrambled in and a few ladles of seasoned oil were added. An almost obscene amount of scallions that had been bathed in a rice batter went on top. Interestingly, the pan used is flat, but it rests on the flame at an almost 45-degree angle, making the top of the pan further from the incredible heat. Each portion of the oyster and egg scramble was no larger than a side plate, and it was topped off with some spiralized radish, which was unexpectedly warm in temperature.

Rather than the typical chile crisp, a generous squirt of a chile sauce was used to finish the dish. It was a cross between the delicious South East Asian sweet chile sauce you might find at a Chinese takeout place in the West, ketchup, and a little sriracha for color. There is a chile sauce from Taichung, Taiwan called *dongquan* or *dung chiua* (東泉) that is an incredibly close match if you can find it.

¼ cup (40 g) rice flour
½ teaspoon salt
½ teaspoon ground white pepper
¼ cup (60 ml) water
5 scallions, finely chopped
10–12 small oysters, shucked, or 2 x 3 oz (85 g) cans of oysters
2 eggs
1–2 tablespoons chile sauce, plus extra to serve
Neutral oil, for frying
Sesame oil, for drizzling
Grated or spiralized daikon, to serve

Put the rice flour into a bowl and season with the salt and white pepper. Add enough of the water to make a batter the consistency of pouring cream or crêpe batter. Add the scallions to the batter, then set aside.

Heat a drizzle of oil in a frying pan over high heat and fry the oysters for 10–15 seconds on each side. Crack in the eggs and scramble them with a spatula, then quickly add the scallion rice batter and continue to stir-fry vigorously for 1 minute until the batter has turned into a scramble. Add the chile sauce and a drizzle of sesame oil and stir until combined.

Serve with some daikon and an extra spoonful of chile sauce.

海蛎煎

Eggs and Some Meat

Jidan Hanbao

鸡蛋汉堡

Egg and Pork Burger
Makes 4

4 oz (120 g) ground pork
2 tablespoons water
1 teaspoon ground white pepper
1 teaspoon light soy sauce
1 scallion, finely chopped
4–5 wood ear mushrooms, soaked and
     finely chopped
4 eggs
Neutral oil, for brushing
Tianmianjiang or chile oil, to serve

For the batter
2 cups (250 g) all-purpose flour
¾ cup (180 ml) water
A pinch of salt
½ teaspoon ground white pepper
1 teaspoon baking powder
1 egg

This "burger" is really a pancake batter puck containing a fried egg and a smidgen of pork flavored with white pepper. The exterior is brushed with a choice of sauces, from *tianmianjiang* or ketchup to strawberry jam. If you feel that this is somewhat familiar, then it might be that you are a fan of a McDonald's sausage and egg McMuffin. I first encountered this breakfast snack at the breakfast market in Qingdao, Shandong province, where it was one of the most popular stalls, but you can find it virtually all over China, particularly close to universities.

A custom pan is really essential here. It is a product of the type of quiet innovation that I witness all the time, ticking over in the background of Chinese food culture. I am in awe of the way in which rudimentary tools for home decoration or construction purposes are co-opted for other uses. It still makes me smile even after many years. A paint scraper makes an excellent spatula, a pair of pliers a fine handle for a frying pan and a shovel is perfect for those really big batches of fried rice. A quick search online for an "egg burger pan" will bring up something with four compartments that will perfectly replicate this recipe for home use.

First, prepare the batter. Combine all the ingredients in a bowl and whisk together to make a thick batter. Set aside to rest.

Combine the pork, water, white pepper, soy sauce, scallion, and mushrooms in a bowl and set aside.

Heat the egg burger pan over medium heat, then brush each of the molds with a little oil. Crack an egg into each hole and cook just until they free themselves or until they are easy enough to flip without runny white going everywhere. Flip them over and cook for another minute.

With a spatula or spoon, lift the eggs up and pour in enough batter to half-fill the molds. Place the eggs back on top, then spoon a quarter of the meat mixture onto each egg.

Cook until the batter forms a crust, then lift up the whole thing and pour in enough batter to fill the mold halfway. Flip the other half on top, creating the sandwich.

Brush the tops of the burgers with a little oil and continue to cook on both sides until golden brown.

Brush the burger with tianmianjiang (my personal favorite) or with some chile oil and devour.

209

Jiaozi Dumplings

This chapter focuses on the delicate, salubrious little parcels that we would call dumplings in English. However, as with the breads and noodles chapters, no one term in Mandarin or Cantonese will ever comfortably cover all expressions or styles.

Dumplings also sit at a strange categorization crossroads between noodles and bread. They lack the portability of bread, but are filled in the same way as many *baozi*. You'll need to be sitting at a table using chopsticks, a spoon, or both, like noodles, but rather than always being boiled in water, they are occasionally pan-fried or steamed.

Jiaozi (饺子), *guotie* (锅贴), *huntun* (馄饨), and *chaoshou* (抄手) are just some of the names used to describe a thin-skinned wrapper encapsulating a filling. In American English the name "pot sticker" is a direct translation of guotie, which literally means "pot stick."

Linguist, physicist, and anthropologist Anthony Zee (sadly no relation) describes the relationship between Chinese food and the written word in his book *Swallowing Clouds*. The Cantonese term for wonton is *yun tun* (雲吞), to "swallow clouds," which sets

the tone for how many Chinese food names arise from poetry, homonyms, or simple comedic observation. In Sichuan dialect, *chaoshou* means to fold your arms, which makes sense when you see these dumplings in their raw state, like someone stubborn or fed up.

Personally, I think *jiaozi* is a better overarching term, being the most neutral in its definition and translation into English and the one that is used and recognized across the widest geographic range in China. This is why I have used this term to define this chapter.

Like noodles, dumplings are full of symbolism. Particularly in the north, jiaozi are made for the Spring Festival (Lunar New Year) because they are a symbol of optimism and their production is best suited to family gatherings with some friendly competition. The category is also incredibly broad, with styles ranging from technical, exact, and delicately pleated, to smushed together between two hands. It's not even essential that they're sealed (see Beijing Guotie, page 224).

Jiaozi Pi

饺子皮

Dumpling Wrapper Dough
Makes 15 wrappers

2 cups (250 g) all-purpose flour
½ cup (125 ml) warm water

Combine the flour and water in a bowl and use a pair of chopsticks to bring it together into a ragged dough.

Using your hands, bring it together further until you have a smooth ball, then tip it out onto a clean work surface and knead for 5–7 minutes until firm.

Cover the dough with the bowl you used to mix, then set aside for 30 minutes.

Use this time to prepare whatever filling you are making.

When the dough is soft and supple, poke your finger through the middle to make what will look like a giant bagel. Stretch the ring of dough larger and then make a cut to create a sausage that is the same thickness at the middle as it is at the end.

Next, portion the dough into pieces. The size of your dumplings really just depends on how big you want to make them. Ideally, they should be no larger than two bites, but at the same time, if you make them too small you will spend half your day assembling dumplings. An average-sized jiaozi will use around ¾–1 oz (20–25 g) of dough, so perhaps weigh the first piece to get an understanding of size.

You can of course cut nuggets of dough off the long sausage as you go, or, like many restaurants, tear pieces off using your thumb as a measure.

Some quick kitchen math will minimize waste, so I suggest weighing your dough and filling and working out the most efficient way to use up both. It is always better to be left with more filling than dough. Dry and brittle dough that has been left out is unsuitable to use, so keep your wrappers covered with some plastic as you work. If you have leftover dough, it's best not to store it, but to repurpose it for other dishes. Leftover filling can be cooked (if raw) and used as a topping for noodles or rice.

This is a basic recipe that will serve you well for almost any dumpling. While there are certainly local variations all over the place, a firm but soft, pliable, and delicate skin is essential.

How dry the air is or how old the flour is will have a minor impact on your dough, but nothing you can't correct in the bowl. The basic premise is two parts flour to one part water. Some like to use boiling water and incorporate it at the start with chopsticks, but I prefer to use something a little cooler, 122–140°F (50–60°C), or the same temperature as a very hot bath.

The vast majority of all-purpose flours from around the world have a 10 percent protein content and most will work here without any issues, so don't worry too much.

Any leftover dough can also be used to make crispy shards for adding to a Jianbing (see page 78) or for crushing and topping literally any noodle dish. Just roll the dough very thin, cut into 4 x 4 in (10 x 10 cm) squares, and make a 1½–2 in (4–5 cm) cut in the middle. This will prevent the squares from warping when you deep-fry them. Fry until crisp and then use as you wish.

212

Shaomai

Jiangnan-Style Dumplings
Makes 12 dumplings (serves 3–4)

1¼ cups (150 g) glutinous rice
2⅔ oz (75 g) fatty ground pork (15% fat) or
    1 tablespoon neutral oil
3½ oz (100 g) smoked tofu, finely diced
2⅔ oz (75 g) chestnut mushrooms, finely diced
1 tablespoon light soy sauce
1 tablespoon dark soy sauce
1 tablespoon sesame oil
A pinch of salt
½ teaspoon ground white pepper
1 x quantity Jiaozi Pi (see page 212)
All-purpose flour, for dusting

There are a lot of different types of *shaomai* (烧卖) across China, Hong Kong, and Asia, and their origins can all be traced back to the northern grasslands of Mongolia. In the provincial capital of Inner Mongolia, Hohhot, they are filled with mutton and heavily flavored with ginger to balance the flavor but also for the root's medicinal properties. The skin is incredibly thin and pinched at the top to create what resembles a delicate peony-style flower.

The concept of shaomai is simple: the filling, mostly meat, is wrapped in a skin but left open at the top, and then steamed. It is dipped into something sharp or balancing like a vinegar or chile sauce. In the Jiangnan region, made up of Shanghai and the immediate vicinity of its neighboring provinces, Zhejiang, Jiangsu, Anhui, and Jiangxi, the predominant filling is sticky glutinous rice, flavored or studded with pork or tiny flecks of smoked tofu. This differs from the perhaps more well-known Cantonese version (see page 248), which uses pork flavored with shrimp. What's more, in the Jiangnan region, the shaomai are generally much larger than those found further north or south. In the Cantonese tradition they're served in steamer baskets as part of a sit-down dim sum meal. Shanghai versions can even be vegan—swap the pork for dried tofu or shiitake mushrooms. The predominantly rice filling also makes this style of shaomai much more filling and inexpensive to buy.

Put the rice into a bowl, cover with water, and set aside to soak for at least 4 hours, or overnight.

Prepare a steamer and line the basket with cheesecloth or parchment paper with some holes poked in it. Discard the soaking water and transfer the rice to the steamer, then cook over medium-high heat for 15 minutes. Remove from the heat but leave the lid on as this will make the rice even stickier.

In a dry frying pan over medium heat, fry the pork, if using, and render out some of the fat. If you're not using the pork, add the oil. Add the tofu and mushrooms and fry for 5 minutes. Add the light and dark soy sauces, sesame oil, and salt and pepper. Cook for a further 5 minutes.

Add the cooked rice to the pork and mushroom mixture and stir until fully combined. Remove from the heat and leave to cool slightly, then weigh the filling and divide it into 12 equal portions.

Divide the dumpling dough into 12 pieces and, on a lightly floured surface, roll each into a 4 in (10 cm) circle. Take a dumpling wrapper and place a portion of the rice filling in the center. Bring the sides up around the filling and shape it into a rough cone shape but don't seal it at the top. You want it looking like a little rice volcano. Flatten the bottom so that it stands up. Repeat until all the filling is used up.

Prepare a fresh steamer as above and steam the dumplings over high heat for 10 minutes until the wrapper is cooked. Allow to cool slightly before serving.

214

烧卖

Xiao Jiaozi

小饺子

Small Jiaozi from Sichuan Province

Makes 25–30 dumplings (serves 2–3)

While *jiaozi* (饺子) might be one of the most well-known types of dumpling in the world, there are countless variations across China that all fall under the same name. In the countryside of Sichuan, about 100 miles (160 km) west of Chengdu, a small restaurant prepares thousands of "small jiaozi" every day. What is so curious about these is their construction.

The skin is on the thick side and is cut into circles from a sheet rather than rolled out individually. Texturally, the filling is somewhat similar to a Fuzhou fish ball or Shantou beef ball, with their bouncy "QQ" texture. This texture is achieved by whipping and stretching the meat proteins, which makes it sticky and chewy. The filling is not sealed, either, but looks somewhat like a wedge of orange. How does the filling not fall out when its cooked? What a unique design, and how on earth did they come up with it?

As I stood watching them being made, I observed their secret: they're frozen before being boiled, which helps maintain their integrity.

217

The dumplings are served with a sauce very similar to that prepared for Tianshui Mian (see page 24) but with a more pronounced sweetness than I had tried in the cities. The great benefits of this style are its make-ahead approach and its lack of fussy pleating that can be so off-putting for perfectionists. It was one of the most immediately delicious dishes I ate while researching this book and I am so happy that it is here for you to try.

Xiao Jiaozi

9 oz (250 g) ground pork
1 tablespoon light soy sauce
A pinch of salt
A pinch of ground white pepper
1 garlic clove, finely chopped
1 thumb-sized piece of fresh root ginger, finely
    chopped
1 x quantity Jiaozi Pi (see page 212)
All-purpose flour, for dusting
3–4 tablespoons Tianshui Mian sauce per
    serving (see page 24)
Toasted white sesame seeds, to garnish

Combine the pork, soy sauce, salt, white pepper,
garlic, and ginger in a food processor or stand
mixer and blend until you can see the texture
becoming somewhat stretchy and gluey. Scrape
out into a bowl and set aside. This can be also
done by hand using the claw technique described
on page 92, or even in a large enough mortar
and pestle.

On a lightly floured surface, roll out the dough
into a sheet about ⅛ in (3 mm) thick. Dust the top
lightly with flour so that the wrappers don't stick
when you stack them. Use a cutter around 1½ in
(4 cm) to cut out as many circles as you can,
stacking them as you go.

Take a circle of dough and place a scant teaspoon
of the pork filling in the middle. Pinch the dough
at the 12 o'clock and 6 o'clock positions and,
using a small knife or spatula, shape the dumpling
like a wedge of orange, pinching the corners and
smoothing off the top. Continue until all the filling
is used up.

Place the dumplings on a baking sheet lined with
parchment paper, then transfer to the freezer
and freeze until solid. Overnight is best.

Bring a large pot or wok of water to a boil and cook
the dumplings from frozen for 6–7 minutes. Add a
cup of cold water and bring to a boil again. Cook
for a further 4–5 minutes until the dumplings rise
to the top and float on the surface of the water.

Put a few tablespoons of the sauce into each
bowl and add the dumplings. Sprinkle over some
sesame seeds, stir, and serve immediately.

219

Xinjiang Baopi Baozi

Xinjiang Thin-Skinned Dumplings
Makes 8–10 dumplings (serves 2)

For all the dumplings and *baozi* available in Han Chinese culture, there is nearly always an equivalent in the Muslim areas of China that swaps out any pork products for lamb or beef. For example, you can make a Sheng Jian Bao (see page 99) and swap out the pork for beef or lamb if you want to make it halal and it will not only work, but it will be utterly delicious, too.

These "thin-skinned" dumplings are dusted with freshly cracked black pepper and ground cumin before serving, which I feel sets them apart in aroma and flavor. I visited a breakfast restaurant in Wulumuqi that served these alongside a clear beef broth noodle soup, Qing Tang Mian (see page 42), which was finished in the bowl with chopped raw garlic and zingy chiles.

The table was packed with dishes, a fried bread, and fluffy baozi filled with shredded pumpkin (page 118) and thigh joints of boiled beef from the soup with a sharp knife to hack off what meat was left.

It occurred to me that morning that the distinctive aroma of soy sauce was also missing. In Xinjiang, the primary salting agent is just that, salt. Use your best-quality salt and make sure your meat has a generous fat content. The result will be a juicy, gravy-like sauce inside the dumpling. I use Shanxi mature vinegar to serve—it has a malty, woody, aged aroma that gives background to the other intense aromatics rather than clashing with them.

→

新疆薄皮包子

Xinjiang Baopi Baozi

1 lb 5 oz (600 g) fatty lamb (consider using
    cheaper cuts like flank, neck, or breast)
1 onion, finely diced
2 heaped teaspoons salt
1 tablespoon cumin seeds (or ground cumin)
1 x quantity Jiaozi Pi (see page 212)
All-purpose flour, for dusting
Freshly ground black pepper, to serve
Shanxi mature vinegar, to serve

First, prepare the meat. The traditional method
is to use two cleavers, oscillating back and forth
to chop the meat into tiny pieces. This tenderizes
the meat as well, and avoids it being ground too
finely. You want it chunky so that the end result is a
delicate, moist filling rather than a solid nugget
of meat.

Alternatively, use a single large kitchen knife and
take your time. Just don't be tempted to use a
food processor.

Transfer the meat to a bowl and add the diced
onion and salt. Stir, then set aside while you
prepare everything else.

Toast the cumin seeds in a dry frying pan over
medium heat for 4–5 minutes until fragrant,
shaking the pan or moving them around with a
spoon so they don't catch and burn.

Once toasted, tip the seeds onto a plate and allow
to cool, then grind into a fine powder using a spice
grinder or mortar and pestle.

These dumplings are slightly larger than a typical
jiaozi. You will need around 1 oz (30 g) dough for
each one. Roll out a piece of dough into a circle
on a lightly floured surface and spoon a generous
tablespoon of the meat into the middle. The
sealing style here is very casual—just fold the
sides up and then pinch shut. Repeat with the
remaining dough and filling.

Prepare a steamer and line the basket with
parchment paper with some holes poked in it.
Steam the dumplings for 10–12 minutes over a
rolling boil, then remove from the heat and leave
them in the steamer with the lid on for an extra
3–4 minutes to ensure they're cooked through.
Serve with a dusting of cumin, some freshly
ground black pepper, and vinegar for dipping.

The chef at Man Kou Xiang Zao Can in Turpan, Xinjiang. She makes a delicious bowl of qing tang mian.

Beijing Guotie

锅贴

Beijing Pot Stickers
Two Ways
Makes 30 dumplings (serves 2–3)

The name *guotie* (锅贴) is where the American English name pot sticker comes from, *guo* (锅) meaning a pot or cooking pan, and *tie* (贴) meaning "to stick." The legend goes that during the early Song Dynasty, the Emperor Taizu walked into the imperial kitchens after following a delicious aroma. On asking the name of the dumplings frying in the pan, the chef was too stunned to speak. The emperor casually answered his own question and named them guotie.

In Shanghai, they make them like a jumbo-sized *jiaozi*, a sealed half-moon shaped dumpling that has the juicy interior of a *xiao long bao* with a crispy bottom. Unfortunately, I never found a shop that I liked, always finding them a bit too greasy for my taste.

However, in Beijing (and the north of China in general) they are a totally different thing altogether. A dumpling wrapper is rolled into an oval and the filling is added like a small sausage, with the top pinched together and the ends open like an Italian *cannolo*. They are pan-fried with a mixture of starch and water, which creates the signature crunchy texture that requires you to scrape them from the pan. They also fill them with more than just pork and one of my favorites is scrambled eggs and garlic chives.

In Beijing, the portion sizes are also notably larger, with 15–20 per serving, I have absolutely no problem at all finishing a plate of them. They are best eaten with a side of vinegar mixed a small spoon of chile crisp to dip.

224

2 x quantities Jiaozi Pi (see page 212)
2 teaspoons cornstarch
Scant ½ cup (100 ml) cold water
All-purpose flour, for dusting
Neutral oil, for frying

For the egg and garlic chive filling
1 tablespoon neutral oil
3 eggs, beaten
10½ oz (300 g) garlic chives (or scallions),
     finely chopped
2 tablespoons light soy sauce
½ teaspoon salt
½ teaspoon ground white pepper
1 tablespoon sesame oil

For the pork filling
9 oz (250 g) ground pork
1¾ oz (50 g) garlic chives (or scallions),
     finely chopped
2 tablespoons light soy sauce
½ teaspoon salt
½ teaspoon ground white pepper
1 tablespoon sesame oil
2 tablespoons water

To serve
Zhenjiang vinegar
Chile Crisp (see page 282, or use store-bought)

First, prepare the fillings.

For the egg filling, heat the oil in a frying pan over medium heat and scramble the eggs until you have a dry scramble. Leave to cool, then finely chop the egg and transfer to a bowl. Add the remaining ingredients and stir well to combine.

For the pork filling, combine all the ingredients in a bowl and use your hand in a claw shape (see page 92) to stir the ingredients into a smooth mixture.

To assemble the dumplings, portion the dough into 1 oz (25 g) pieces, then roll out the pieces on a lightly floured surface into a shape that is slightly rectangular or oval. Spread a generous amount of filling along the length, then bring the sides up and pinch it together, leaving the ends open. Repeat until all the dough or fillings are used up.

225

Mix together the cornstarch and water in a small bowl and set aside.

Heat a little oil in a frying pan over medium heat and add the dumplings. You want them to be quite snug up against each other, so fit as many as you can. Fry the dumplings gently for 8–10 minutes until the bottoms are a light golden brown.

Increase the heat a little, then give the cornstarch mixture a stir and pour it into the pan around the dumplings. Give it a jiggle so that it disperses among the dumplings, and cover with a lid. The dumplings are ready once all the water has been absorbed and the bottoms are a deep golden brown. The starch will have created a uniform crust.

Serve the dumplings bottom side up with a side of vinegar and some chile crisp.

Jiucai Hezi

Fried Pastries with Garlic Chives
Makes 6 pastries

These pretty little pies are a favorite of Northeast China, especially the provinces of Shandong, Henan, and Shanxi during Chinese New Year. They have a delightfully crimped edge that is reminiscent of empanadas or *shapale* from Tibet. One of the unique characteristics of these chive pockets is their generous filling—they are simply rammed full.

228

The star of the show is *jiucai* (韭菜), or garlic chives, a long, flat, green, grass-like vegetable that is oniony and garlicky, with a delicate herbaceous flavor. Here it is combined with dry scrambled eggs, and on occasion you can also find small pieces of ultra-thin rice vermicelli or very thin slices of smoked tofu in the mix. In Shanghai, you'll find them made by street sellers tucked down alleyways or in residential compounds to avoid being moved along by the local government. Many contemporary recipes will lightly fry them, but you should fry them in plenty of oil in my opinion. The skin takes on a blistered appearance and the edges, rather than being pale and doughy, are properly cooked.

The dough is simple enough to make, just flour and hot water, so not too dissimilar to making a regular dumpling wrapper. There is minimal kneading and no layering involved and the majority of the preparation goes into the filling.

For the dough
3⅓ cups (400 g) all-purpose flour
A pinch of salt
1 cup (250 ml) boiling water
Neutral oil, for coating and frying

For the filling
3½ oz (100 g) rice vermicelli
4 eggs, beaten
12 oz (350 g) garlic chives, finely chopped
Salt and black pepper
Neutral oil, for frying

First, make the dough. Combine the flour and salt in a bowl, then slowly pour over the boiling water, stirring with a pair of chopsticks to bring it together into a loose and scraggy mass. Using your hands, bring it together into a smooth ball and knead for 7–8 minutes until smooth. Coat with a little oil, then cover and set aside to rest for 30 minutes.

Bring a large pot of water to a boil and cook the rice vermicelli according to the package instructions, but remove them 1–2 minutes before the instructions advise. Transfer to a bowl of iced water to stop the cooking. Dry on paper towels, then chop into small pieces the same size as the garlic chives.

Heat a little oil in a frying pan over medium heat and scramble the eggs until you have a dry scramble. Leave to cool, then finely chop the egg and transfer to a bowl.

Add the rice vermicelli and garlic chives to the egg, season with salt and pepper, and mix thoroughly.

Weigh the dough and divide it into six equal-sized pieces, then roll each piece into a large circle, about ⅛ in (3 mm) thick.

Divide the filling among the dough circles, placing a huge mound in the middle. Fold the dough in half and firmly seal around the edge. If you like, create a braided edge by folding the edge over itself in one corner and repeating along the sealed edge.

Heat 1 in (2½ cm) oil in a frying pan over medium-high heat. Gently fry the dumplings on each side until golden brown and the skin is bumpy and blistered.

Drain on paper towels, then eat while warm.

Xiao Huntun

小馄饨

Little Wontons

Makes 20–25 wontons (serves 2)

These little dumplings are like swallowing clouds. The Cantonese name for wonton comes from *yun tun* (云吞), literally "to swallow clouds," which has now been transliterated into Mandarin in a rather mundane way.

When they are finished cooking, they float to the top of the water with their frilly and delicate tails and bob on the surface like clouds. Here again the north/south divide comes into play. In southern China and Hong Kong, they're small and dainty with a meager amount of meat—usually two to three will fit on a soup spoon. In the north (as with almost everything) they are larger, with a more generous filling. The skins are slippery and thin and they can be served in noodle soup, too.

In Shanghai, they are most common for breakfast. The soup, if you can call it that, is a barely flavored water with a few strips of egg omelet, some seaweed, and a spoonful of melted lard. Only in the fanciest restaurants are you served a soup made from pork bones. The delicacy here is in the wonton, not the soup.

In China, dumpling wrappers are graded by thickness. In the West this is almost never the case, but through trial and error you want to find the thinnest possible. The filling should be simple, pork with just one pairing, whether it's scallion, pumpkin, garlic, chives, or ginger.

The sealing technique couldn't be easier, either. Use a pair of chopsticks to place a teaspoon of the filling in the middle of the wrapper, then, without removing the chopsticks, press the skin around the end of the chopstick with your free hand and then pull it out. You will have a dumpling that has a ball of filling with the excess forming a small skirt.

9 oz (250 g) ground pork
2 teaspoons Shaoxing wine
A pinch of salt
A pinch of MSG
3½ tablespoons water
1 packet of square wonton wrappers
2 tablespoons light soy sauce
2 scallions (green part only), finely chopped
2 teaspoons lard
½ teaspoon ground white pepper

Combine the pork, Shaoxing wine, salt, and MSG
in a bowl and mix well, then add the water and
combine into a smooth paste.

Take a wrapper and, using chopsticks, place about
a teaspoon of filling in the middle. Gather the
wrapper around the ends of the chopsticks and
seal it with your hand. Slide out the chopsticks.
Pinch to seal the wonton.

Repeat until all the meat is used up. Any leftover
wrappers can be stored in the freezer.

Divide the soy sauce, scallions, and lard between
two bowls and add a pinch of white pepper to
each.

Bring a large pot of water to a boil and cook the
wontons for 2–3 minutes until they float, then
remove them with a slotted spoon and place in the
bowls. Cover with a little freshly boiled water to
create a broth, then serve.

Hongyou Chaoshou 红油抄手

Red Oil Dumplings
Makes 20–25 dumplings (serves 3–4)

In a rather unassuming suburb of Chengdu is an unusual restaurant. In China, it's not uncommon to find restaurants inside residential buildings (often operating illegally), but as you approach Ba Er Gan Haijiao Chaoshou, you realize there isn't even a door. Climbing a makeshift staircase through an open window, inside you find a small but bustling restaurant housed in a regular apartment.

This is by no means a hidden gem—it's very popular with locals. I am handed a slip of paper with a handwritten number on it and I wait my turn to order. They serve all the classics, but are most famous for their *hongyou chaoshou* (红油抄手), or red oil dumplings. "Chaoshou" is a verb, meaning to fold your arms, but in Sichuan dialect it refers to these dumplings, a detail that becomes apparent when you see them in their raw state. Through some food anthropomorphism you can imagine a stubborn looking person sitting with their arms crossed.

Chaoshou differ from *jiaozi* in that they are always served in a soup or sauce—either chicken soup, hot and sour soup or, my favorite, chile oil.

In Chengdu, as with noodles, portions are generally much smaller than Shanghai and Beijing. A bowl of chaoshou will typically contain a maximum of eight dumplings, whereas elsewhere it would be 12–15. The smaller size allows you to snack or try multiple dishes from a menu.

Unfortunately, the restaurant has now moved around the corner into more respectable premises, with a regular door.

→

Hongyou Chaoshou

2 scallions
1 thumb-sized piece of fresh root ginger
3½ tablespoons water
9 oz (250 g) fatty ground pork (15% fat)
1 egg
1 teaspoon cornstarch
1 tablespoon oyster sauce (optional)
1 tablespoon light soy sauce
1 packet of square wonton wrappers

To serve (per portion)
1 teaspoon lard
1 teaspoon light soy sauce
½ teaspoon ground Sichuan pepper
A pinch of granulated sugar
2 tablespoons Chile Crisp (see page 282, or use
    store-bought)
1 tablespoon thinly sliced scallion greens

234

Put the scallions, ginger, and water into a blender or food processor and blend until smooth, then pass through a sieve to remove any large pieces. Set aside.

Put the pork, egg, cornstarch, oyster sauce, if using, and soy sauce into a bowl and add a quarter of the ginger and onion liquid. Use your hand in a claw shape to mix the meat in one direction and one direction only. This will help whip the protein structure, creating a light and delicate texture. This process is called *shang jin* (上劲). Set a timer for 15 minutes and hand whip the meat until you have a smooth paste, every couple of minutes adding a little bit more of the ginger and onion liquid until it has all been absorbed. Set aside to rest for 15 minutes.

When you're ready to assemble the dumplings, take a wrapper and place it in your hand in a diamond shape. Using chopsticks, place a teaspoon of the filling in the middle. Fold the diamond in half from the bottom up and press it closed tightly with your hands. Turn the dumpling so the top point is facing you. Take the left and the right point and cross them over each other tightly, pressing them together.

Continue until you run out of filling or wrappers—any leftovers of either can be frozen.

Put the serving ingredients, except the scallion greens, into bowls.

Bring a large pot of water to a boil and add the dumplings. When the water comes back up to a boil, add a cup of cold tap water to cool the water. Bring the water back up to a boil and once the dumplings are floating, divide them between the bowls.

Add a small splash of the cooking water to each bowl to make a soup, then garnish with the scallion greens.

Dumplings

Xiao Long Bao

小笼包

Shanghainese Soup Dumplings

Makes 18 dumplings (serves 2)

This is the global superstar of all Shanghainese dishes. The name *xiao long bao* (小笼包) translates simply as "small basket bao," but there are actually many styles depending on where in Jiangsu, Zhejiang, or even Fujian province you are. The Wuxi style, found at Shan Shan in Jing'an District, Shanghai, are exceptionally large, with six in a serving compared to the usual eight or ten. They are served with a sharp vinegar to balance the sweetness.

The Suzhou style, similar to Wuxi in taste, are flavored with soy and sugar but are smaller. In the city of Quanzhou on the Fujian coast, I was once served a basket of the cutest baby-sized leavened baozi, but instead of the typical pleating on the top, they were spherical, with the pleat on the bottom.

Head down to south Shanghai, to Wu You Xian, and you will find one of the most extensive menus of hairy crab xiao long baos, with different sections of crab meat, the leg, brown meat, and pure roe paired with different vinegars to balance the intensity or fattiness. One of the highlights of their menu is the palate cleanser—a whole puréed lemon with a touch of sugar. A fresh, bright, bitter, citrusy shot with an almost oily finish that is totally sublime.

For the absolute best xiao long bao, there are really no substitutes possible. The ceremony of seeing them made is why most people, even the Chinese, rarely make them at home. They are technically quite challenging, and every element has to be prepared fresh. For example, you cannot use store-bought dumpling wrappers, they are just too dry and brittle. And you shouldn't use gelatin powder for the soup, as it has the wrong consistency and taste. Take your time to prepare the various elements in advance and gather some friends and family to make light work of production.

Xiao long bao also freeze very well. Pleat them and place them on a lined baking sheet that fits in your freezer. Once frozen, they can be kept in a plastic bag in the freezer for up to 6 months. Cook them from frozen, giving them an extra 3 minutes of cooking time.

236

Xiao Long Bao

For the pork soup

1 lb 2 oz (500 g) pork skin, cut into chunks
2 scallions
1 thumb-sized piece of fresh root ginger
3 tablespoons Shaoxing wine
A pinch of salt
½ teaspoon ground white pepper

For the dough

2 cups (250 g) dumpling flour, plus extra
    for dusting
Scant ½ cup (100 ml) water
A pinch of salt

For the filling

2 scallions
1 thumb-sized piece of fresh root ginger
7 oz (200 g) pork belly, finely ground, or fatty
    ground pork (15% fat)
1 teaspoon cornstarch
2 teaspoons light soy sauce
1 egg yolk

To serve

Zhenjiang vinegar
Fresh root ginger, finely julienned

Prepare the pork soup a day in advance.

Put the pork skin into a pot and cover with water. Bring to a boil and cook for 10 minutes, then discard the water and remove the skin.

Finely chop the skin, add it back to the pot with all the other ingredients, and add enough water just to cover the skin. Simmer over low heat for 2 hours. (Alternatively, you could cook this in a pressure cooker for 25 minutes.)

Strain the skin through a fine sieve into a container, then cover and chill in the fridge overnight until the mix is solid and gelatinous. This will keep for a week in the fridge or in the freezer for six months.

Next, prepare the dough. Combine the flour with the water and salt and bring it together with your hands into a smooth dough that comes away from the sides of the bowl. Knead for 10 minutes, then cover and set aside to rest for 30 minutes.

Meanwhile, prepare the filling. Put the scallions and ginger into a blender or food processor and blend until smooth, then pass through a sieve to remove any large pieces.

Combine the pork, onion and ginger liquid, cornstarch, soy sauce, and egg yolk in a bowl. Use your hand in a claw shape to mix the meat in one direction and one direction only. This will help whip the protein structure, creating a light and delicate texture.

Remove the solidified pork soup from the container and either mash it or finely chop it, then incorporate it into the pork filling mixture. Set aside.

Prepare a steamer and line two steamer baskets with parchment paper with some holes poked in it.

Roll the dough into a long sausage, then divide it into roughly 18 pieces. Roll out each piece on a lightly floured surface into a circle about 4 in (10 cm) across. The key here is to roll the edges thinner than the center. It might seem logical to use the rolling pin in an outwards motion to make them thinner but the opposite is true. Position the rolling pin at the edge of the round and apply pressure as you roll the edge towards the center, turning the wrapper with your other hand.

Place a teaspoon of the filling in the center of one of the pieces and pleat the dumpling closed. Hold the dumpling in your left hand and, using your right, pinch the 12 o'clock to the 11, 10, 9, and so on until the edges are gathered back around to the starting position. While the right hand is gathering the edges up, the left hand is slowly turning the dumpling in a clockwise motion. If you have an excessive amount of dough on the top, don't be afraid to pinch it off.

Place directly in the prepared steamer basket. Repeat with the remaining filling.

Steam the dumplings over vigorously boiling water for 8–10 minutes until cooked through, then serve immediately with vinegar and ginger mixed together in small bowls.

Dumplings

Haozi Baba

蒿子粑粑

Artemisia-Stuffed Rice Cakes
Makes 8–10 dumplings (serves 4–5)

This recipe was given to me by my friend Joe Gong. It forms part of a two-part breakfast made for him by his grandmother in Hunan (see page 266).

These are a chewy rice cake flavored with artemisia, also known in English as wormwood, a common flavoring in vermouths and more famously known as the active ingredient in absinthe. It has been used for its medicinal properties in both Western and Chinese cultures for centuries with no reports of any side effects. It has a potent, sage-like flavor with a strong bitterness that is tempered by a brief blanching in hot water.

This recipe has a filling of crushed soy beans and brown sugar, but you can fill them with anything, from nuts to meat fillings you would use for dumplings—just don't be tempted to overfill them. You can prepare them in advance and freeze them, ready to be fried or steamed in the morning for a delicious treat at breakfast. If cooking from frozen, add an additional 3–4 minutes to the cooking time.

You can buy artemisia plants online, but you can also use sage as an alternative.

1¾ oz (50 g) soy bean powder (often sold as kinako)
4 tablespoons brown sugar
3½ oz (100 g) artemisia (or sage), leaves picked
Scant ½ cup (100 ml) water
2 cups (250 g) glutinous rice flour
Neutral oil, for frying

Combine the soy bean flour and sugar in a bowl and set aside.

241

Bring a large pot of water to a boil and blanch the artemisia leaves for 30–45 seconds. Remove and allow the leaves to cool. This will soften the texture and remove the harsh bitterness of the artemisia.

Finely chop the leaves or blend in a food processor into a smooth paste. Transfer to a bowl with the water and glutinous rice flour and combine with your hands into a smooth dough.

Divide the dough into eight or ten pieces, depending on how large you want the dumplings. Roll each piece into a ball, then poke your thumb into the middle. Gently expand the indent so the ball takes on the shape of a clay cup. Add a tablespoon of the filling to the middle, then bring up the sides and pinch shut. Press it into a patty.

Heat a little oil in a frying pan over low heat, then gently fry the dumplings for 10 minutes on each side. Don't be tempted to cook them too fast or the dough will be undercooked. They will initially stick to even the most seasoned pans, but will eventually self-release.

Yum Cha
Morning Tea

Whole books could be dedicated to the culture of *yum cha* (飲茶) or *zao cha* (早茶). This ritualistic Cantonese act of taking tea with two small dishes was first developed in the cafés and tea houses of Guangdong province but is now an entire spectrum of food and dining culture ingrained in the psyches of millions around the world. *Dim sum* (点心), the name given to the dishes that accompany the tea, literally translates as "touch the heart."

I visited Qian Ji Zao Cha, a rough and ready breakfast place in a small suburb of Guangzhou, the provincial capital of Guangdong province, formerly known at Canton. With self-service tea at the entrance, you order at the hatch and take a seat. Over the course of the meal, the waitress brings around enormous steamer baskets filled with small plates of things like chicken feet with black bean or tripe with ginger that can happily sit in a steamer for some time without overcooking. The rest of the menu is made to order. For research purposes, I ordered nearly the entire menu for a handsome sum of 50RMB (about $7).

This experience represents the lower end of the scale for yum cha, in affordability but also in terms of the pomp and ceremony often associated with it. Over the course of writing this book, I spoke to several friends about their experiences growing up in Guangzhou and Hong Kong, the two spheres of influence over Cantonese cooking. They reminisced about the trolley service at Maxim's (a well-known dim sum restaurant) and the enormity of the tables that were needed to accommodate the many branches of the family tree that would attend the meals. They recalled their favorite dishes, enjoyed as a trade-off for having to sit next to a difficult auntie or uncle.

Historically, in Guangdong province, people ate twice a day: late in the morning before noon and before sunset. Teahouses were never substitutes for meals but were there to fill the gaps. The food was secondary to the act of drinking tea, which allowed for balance in line with a Taoist philosophy. This philosophy posits that humans and nature are the same and we should only consume simple and unprocessed foods, embrace vegetarianism, and fast often. Overconsumption is noted as a barrier to health and longevity; two bites is often enough.

Chinese culture also derives many food pairings from the medicinal properties of ingredients. Long before

Morning Tea

it was recognized in the West, China understood that green tea inhibits the absorption of fatty lipids in the intestine. It is probable that, consumed on a regular basis, green tea reduces the overall caloric value of many foods. Teahouses were places to do business or chat with friends, similar to how we use coffee shops today. The idea that you would have dim sum for dinner is unimaginable in the same way that it would be strange to go to Starbucks for your evening meal.

Following the post-revolutionary decline of Guangzhou and the boom of Hong Kong, however, the colony city assumed the title "Heaven of Delicacies" and overtook Guangzhou as the center of Cantonese cuisine.

The book *Changing Chinese Foodways in Asia* by David Y. H. Wu and Chee Beng Tan contains a great essay by Siumi Maria Tam that explores the perceptions of Hong Kong as a city without its own identity, instead merely an economic outpost of the British Empire right up to the 1970s. When the handover back to China loomed, discussions of a collective future began, with fears of being "swallowed whole by China" becoming a daily news topic. While teahouses have existed in Hong Kong for over 150 years, recent diversification has taken the dynamics and social context of yum cha in a different direction and to new audiences.

The Hong Kong expansion and, some might say, globalization of dim sum in the second half of the twentieth century saw the role of tea take second place. As the menu grew to incorporate a wider range of tastes and styles, other non-Cantonese dishes started to appear.

Shanghainese, Hakka, or even Japanese influences and waiters wearing bow ties helped to distinguish Hong Kong as a classy destination. Dim sum is now less about a delicate touch of the heart than a fully formed sophisticated dining experience.

The rules have been adapted and now help to define yum cha as separate to other Hong Kong establishments like *cha chaan teng* (a café that is a fusion of Hong Kong and colonial British tastes) or *dai pai dong* (literally "big licence stalls," outdoor street vendors noted for their physically larger trading licence). There is now an accepted etiquette to the yum cha experience that most follow: pouring tea requires you to tap two fingers on the table for gratitude, the eldest at the table takes priority on first choice, there is a silent signal for the teapot to be refilled and reaching excessively for the last morsel is an acknowledged faux pas.

It can go beyond this, too. To serve someone else the last dumpling is seen as a sign of polite submission and respect. And it has become common practice to pretend to go to the toilet only to pay for the entire bill while everyone else fights it out. The drive to modernize yum cha combined with the nostalgia for the traditional has now filtered back into the mainland, with Hong Kong-style yum cha a set style that commands higher prices.

This chapter presents some essential dishes as well as personal favorites that make up a dim sum meal regardless of what side of the border you are on.

245

Wu Gok

芋
角

Taro Puffs
Makes 9 (serves 3)

These frilly, bird's-nest-looking nuggets are so glorious in their retro charm, presented in paper muffin cups that offset their chaotic appearance, that no dim sum table is complete without them. I remember having them at Lin Heung in Hong Kong with my friend Wilson Fok, who at the time was the dining editor for *Tatler Hong Kong*. He was on good terms with both the staff and the menu, knowing exactly what time of day certain dishes would be at their freshest, and without me having to do anything, a procession of food started to arrive on steamer trollies. Lin Heung has now sadly shut down after 100 years with only Maxim's Palace (to my knowledge) still providing trolley service.

Shaped like a rugby ball, this consists of a rich filling wrapped in a combination of steamed taro and wheat starch, which, when deep-fried, creates a surface that resembles pumice stone or a gnarly hay bale. The texture is light, crisp and, most importantly, never greasy.

The filling is a classic mix of pork and shrimp flavored with oyster sauce, but you can also find them filled with mushrooms. If you want to make a vegetarian or vegan version, just swap out the lard in the dough for butter or your preferred vegan substitute.

For the dough
14 oz (400 g) taro, peeled and cubed
⅔ cup (100 g) wheat starch (not all-purpose flour)
2 tablespoons unsalted butter
2 tablespoons lard
A pinch of salt
½ teaspoon ground white pepper
Scant ½ cup (100 ml) boiling water
Neutral oil, for frying

For the filling
9 oz (250 g) ground pork
3½ oz (100 g) peeled raw shrimp, finely chopped
1 tablespoon dried shrimp
2 dried shiitake or chestnut mushrooms
1 garlic clove, finely chopped
2 tablespoons oyster sauce
1 tablespoon dark soy sauce
1 teaspoon sesame oil
A pinch of granulated sugar
1 tablespoon cornstarch
⅔ cups (150 ml) cold water

Morning Tea

First, prepare the dough. Prepare a steamer, then steam the taro over high heat for 20 minutes until soft.

Transfer the taro to a bowl and allow it to cool slightly, then add three-quarters of the wheat starch, the butter, lard, and salt and pepper and mash them together with a potato masher or fork. Add the boiling water and continue to mash, then finish with the remaining starch. The consistency should be like firm mashed potatoes.

Cover and chill in the fridge for at least 30 minutes while you prepare the filling.

Bring a large pot of water to a boil and blanch the pork and raw shrimp for 10 seconds, then drain. This is to remove any unpleasant odors.

Put the dried shrimp into a dry frying pan over medium heat and toast for 3–4 minutes until fragrant. Add the pork and shrimp, mushrooms, garlic, oyster sauce, soy sauce, sesame oil, and sugar and cook for 5 minutes until the shrimp begin to change color.

Stir together the cornstarch and water in a small bowl, then add it to the filling mixture. Continue to cook until you have a thick and glossy sauce coating the filling, about 5 minutes. Transfer to a plate and set aside to cool.

Remove the dough from the fridge and knead it for 1 minute so that it is smooth and pliable. Weigh and divide the dough into nine equal-sized pieces. Do the same with the filling.

Take a piece of dough, flatten it into a disc with your hands, and pile on some of the filling. Make sure to seal it firmly, as you don't want any filling escaping. Repeat with the remaining dough and filling.

Heat 2–2½ in (5–6 cm) oil in a large saucepan, deep frying pan, or wok until it reaches 350°F (180°C).

247

The technique for frying the puffs is somewhat unusual. Gently press three puffs onto a spider strainer. You don't want the puffs to float freely in the oil.

Carefully half-submerge the puffs in the oil for 30 seconds, then continue with a full dunk. The high water content in the dough escapes as steam, which creates the frilly texture but is also volatile and can spit and splash so be careful. If you have a splash guard or oil screen, I suggest you use it. Fry for 4–5 minutes until golden brown, then drain on paper towels.

Repeat with the remaining puffs, then serve in paper muffin cups.

Siu Mai

Cantonese-Style Siu Mai
Makes 20 (serves 4)

3½ oz (100 g) shiitake mushrooms, finely diced (or 1 oz/25 g dried shiitake)
5½ oz (150 g) fatty ground pork (15% fat)
3½ oz (100 g) peeled raw shrimp, finely chopped (don't use cooked shrimp for this)
1 egg
1 tablespoon cornstarch
A pinch of salt
1 teaspoon granulated sugar
1 tablespoon Shaoxing wine
1 teaspoon ground white pepper
1 thumb-sized piece of fresh root ginger, very finely chopped or grated
1 package of round siu mai wrappers
Goji berries, to garnish (optional)
Zhenjiang vinegar, to serve

I have such fond memories of making *siu mai* (烧卖), also spelled *shaomai*, as a child. My father would make them at home, and it was low-skilled enough that my siblings and I were allowed to ham-fistedly make our way through a pile of wrappers.

248

In adult life, I discovered it's common for people to add things like thinly sliced bamboo shoots or water chestnuts to the mix. This is something my family doesn't do, and the first time I experienced it, I spat it out to inspect what was inside my siu mai. Even today I still dislike any additional ingredients in mine.

The filling is otherwise simple, as is the assembly. Two quick notes on the wrappers: make sure they are the yellow variety, made with lye water, and for this recipe, circular wrappers are best.

You can also triple or quadruple this recipe and freeze the siu mai. Place them on a tray lined with parchment paper, making sure they're not touching, then freeze them overnight. Then next day, transfer them to a freezer-proof bag or container and then steam from frozen whenever you fancy.

If you are using dried shiitake mushrooms, put them into a heatproof bowl and cover with boiling water, then leave to rehydrate for 1 hour. Drain (save the mushroom broth for another use) and finely chop.

Combine the mushrooms, pork, shrimp, egg, cornstarch, salt, sugar, Shaoxing wine, white pepper, and ginger in a bowl and use your hand in a claw shape to mix in one direction and one direction only. This will help whip the protein structure and emulsify the meat, creating a light and delicate texture.

Don't be tempted to use a food processor here—the additional chopping will make the filling too smooth and the end texture will be solid and dry rather than open and juicy.

Take a wrapper and place a generous teaspoon of the filling in the middle. Bring the sides up around the filling and leave the top exposed. Press the siu mai down on the table to create a flat bottom and smooth off the top. Repeat until all the filling is used up. Decorate each siu mai with a single goji berry, if using.

Prepare a steamer and line the basket with parchment paper with some holes poked in it. Steam the dumplings in small batches (three or four dumplings per basket) for 12–15 minutes over a rolling boil until cooked through and tender.

Serve immediately with vinegar on the side.

廣式燒賣

Char Siu Bao

Char Siu Pork Buns
Makes 10 buns

Paper-white, steaming hot, and filled with rich, glazed pork in a sweet sauce, these buns are pure perfection and, without any doubt, are my death row dim sum dish.

As a child, I remember walking the streets of Chinatown in Liverpool with my father. We would stop at a residential house on Seel Street, the steps worn smooth from decades of passing customers. Inside the front room was a Cantonese couple selling *char siu bao* (叉烧包). I tried to find it again a few years ago, but the street has been renovated and the shop and couple are long gone.

I was completely unaware of the nuances of regional Chinese food as a child, and I simply ate what was given to me. My grandfather liked a mix of his native Shanghainese cuisine, known for its sweetness, and the Cantonese cooking he had tried on his voyages at sea with the Blue Funnel Line shipping company.

For supremely fluffy buns in the Cantonese style, there is a slight technical divergence from the regular bao dough technique that requires a little more advance preparation.

For the filling
7 oz (200 g) pork belly, cut into small cubes
1 teaspoon light soy sauce
3–4 tablespoons water
2 tablespoons Shaoxing wine
Neutral oil, for frying

For the sauce
½ teaspoon salt
2 tablespoons light soy sauce
2 tablespoons dark soy sauce
3 tablespoons oyster sauce
1 tablespoon granulated sugar
4 tablespoons char siu sauce (I use Lee Kum Kee brand)
1 heaped tablespoon cornstarch
Scant ½ cup (100 ml) cold water

For the dough (part one)
1½ cups (170 g) low-gluten flour or cake flour
¾ cup (170 ml) lukewarm water
¼ oz (7 g) envelope instant yeast

For the dough (part two)
1¼ cups (150 g) low-gluten flour or cake flour, plus extra for dusting
¼ cup (50 g) granulated sugar
¼ oz (7 g) envelope instant yeast
2 tablespoons lard, softened
3 tablespoons distilled white vinegar, for steaming

The day before eating, prepare the filling. Heat a little oil in a frying pan over medium heat and fry the pork for 10–12 minutes until gently browned on the edges. You don't want to render out the fat, so be careful not to cook it over too high a heat. Add the soy sauce, water, and Shaoxing wine and cook for another 4–5 minutes. Remove from the heat and leave to cool, then drain off the cooking liquid and reserve it for the sauce.

For the sauce, combine the reserved cooking liquid from the pork with all the remaining ingredients except the cornstarch and cold water in a pot. Bring to a gentle simmer and cook for 10–12 minutes until glossy.

Stir together the cornstarch and cold water in a small bowl to form a slurry. Add the slurry to the sauce and cook until it thickens to a ketchup-like consistency. Remove from the heat and set aside to cool. Add the cooked pork belly, cover, and refrigerate.

The filling can be refrigerated for 2–3 days in advance of preparing the dough.

On the day of eating, prepare part one of the dough. Combine all the ingredients in a bowl and bring together into a wet dough, almost like a batter, then cover and set aside in a cool, draught-free place for 90 minutes to bubble and become active.

Now prepare part two of the dough. In a stand mixer fitted with the dough hook attachment, combine the first stage dough with all the ingredients from the second (except the vinegar), and knead on a low speed until it comes together into a ball, then increase the speed to medium and knead for 4 minutes.

Transfer the dough to a clean bowl, cover, and set aside to rest for 45 minutes.

Once rested, roll out the dough on a lightly floured surface into a large rectangle and fold it in half. Roll it back to the original size, then repeat this three times. Finally, roll the rectangle into a sausage, weigh it, then cut the dough into 10 equal-sized pieces.

Take a piece of dough and flatten it out so that it is just larger than the palm of your hand. Add a generous tablespoon of the filling to the middle, then close. We are not closing it in a circular motion like a typical bao: imagine a triangle within the circle, with points at 12 o'clock, 4 o'clock, and 8 o'clock. Pinch together the dough at those points towards the middle, to end up with a triangular shaped-bun.

Gently push down in the middle with your finger and in your hand bring the three corners up. Gently pinch them closed at the edges. During the steaming process, the tops of the buns will unfurl, creating the signature three-pointed shape of the most perfect char siu bao.

Prepare a steamer and line the basket with parchment paper with some holes poked in it. Add the 3 tablespoons of vinegar to the water. There is an old wives' tale that says this makes your bao whiter—while I'm not sure it makes much difference, it doesn't feel right not to.

Steam the bao in batches of two or three for 10 minutes, then turn off the heat to allow the residual heat to continue cooking without causing temperature shock to the bao. Allow any leftover bao to cool completely before refrigerating for up to 1 day or freezing for up to 1 month.

251

Morning Tea

Chi Zhi Fengzhao

鼓汁凤爪

Black Bean Chicken Feet

Serves 3–4

The direct translation of this dish is "fermented bean phoenix claws," which gives you some idea of the poetic approach the Chinese take to naming their dishes. However, I feel it somewhat diverts our attention from the almost mundane frugality of the dish. The often-discarded chicken feet are one of the most highly prized ingredients of Asian cooking, but many Westerners find them challenging both in appearance and mouthfeel.

The preparation is not complicated, but there are many stages involved. Luckily, most of it can be done in advance, leaving just the marinade to make before cooking and serving. The various boiling, frying, and soaking stages are to remove any impurities from the feet, soften the texture, and plump them up so they act like a flavor sponge to soak up the marinade. The final product is a star among the rest of the dishes in a Cantonese-style dim sum feast.

It is now not uncommon to find boneless chicken feet in the freezer section of Asian supermarkets in the West. One of the best bar snacks I ever had was deep-fried chicken feet skin. Boil the boneless feet for 15–20 minutes, cool and dry thoroughly, and then deep-fry in oil, seasoning with whatever you like.

10 chicken feet
1 large thumb-sized piece of fresh root
    ginger, sliced
1 tablespoon dark soy sauce
3 garlic cloves, finely chopped
1 tablespoon Chile Crisp (see page 282, or use
    store-bought)
2 tablespoons light soy sauce
1 tablespoon fermented black beans
½ teaspoon ground white pepper
1 teaspoon cornstarch
1 tablespoon sesame oil
Neutral oil, for frying
Thinly sliced red chile, to garnish

Using poultry shears, strong scissors, or a cleaver, cut off the tip of the toes of the chicken feet.

Put the feet into a pot and pour over enough water to cover them, then add the ginger slices and the dark soy sauce. Bring to a boil, then simmer for 20 minutes, carefully removing any scum that floats to the top. Drain and set the feet aside to cool.

Heat enough oil for shallow-frying in a frying pan over medium heat. Fry the feet for 10–12 minutes until golden brown but not crispy. Drain on paper towels.

Transfer the feet to a bowl of cold water and leave to soak for at least 1 hour. You want the skin of the feet to look wrinkly, like when you've been in the bathtub for too long. Once soaked, drain and cut the feet in half lengthways. Set aside in a heatproof bowl.

Fry the garlic, chile crisp, light soy sauce, black beans, and white pepper in a frying pan over medium heat for 5 minutes to release their fragrance. Pour over the chicken feet and stir to coat. Once cool enough to handle, add the cornstarch and use your hands to massage the marinade into the feet. Set aside to marinate for 30 minutes.

Arrange the chicken feet daintily on a plate that will fit inside a bamboo steamer, then steam over high heat for 30 minutes.

Garnish with the sesame oil and a few slices of red chile. Serve immediately.

She Die Jinqian Du

沙嗲金錢肚

Satay, Scallion, and Ginger Tripe
Serves 4

Tripe has something of a sad reputation in much of the West now. A post-war cleansing of British cooking relegated tripe to dog food and it doesn't look like it's in for a renaissance anytime soon.

The Chinese name for honeycomb tripe, *jinqian du* (金钱肚), literally translates as "money belly," because its pattern is reminiscent of ancient Chinese coins, which had a square hole in the middle. The idea is that the more you eat, the richer you become. This recipe generally uses honeycomb tripe, although book tripe, with its frilly pages, can also be substituted.

The tripe is cleaned thoroughly, boiled, and then steamed in a delicate and fragrant sauce. Underneath the tripe you will find chunky batons of steamed daikon radish, which form a sort of structural mound that the tripe is piled on top of, creating a secondary texture.

Be careful not to overcook it—the texture shouldn't be mushy, but rather delicately soft. The perfect vehicle for flavor.

1 lb 2 oz (500 g) honeycomb tripe
¾ cup (100 g) kosher salt
Scant ½ cup (100 ml) white distilled vinegar
2 star anise
2 bay leaves
1 piece of cassia bark
1 teaspoon Sichuan peppercorns
3 tablespoons Shaoxing wine
2 scallions
3 large slices of fresh root ginger
1 tablespoon cornstarch
2 tablespoons satay sauce (Lee Kum Kee brand is classic but Yeo's also make a good one)
1 tablespoon chu hou paste (also Lee Kum Kee)
1 tablespoon abalone sauce (also Lee Kum Kee)
1 teaspoon salt
1 teaspoon granulated sugar
7 oz (200 g) daikon, peeled and cut into batons
1 green chile, sliced
1 red chile, sliced

Regardless of whether you buy bleached or unbleached tripe, you still need to scrub it clean to within an inch of its life. Check every cavity for debris and liberally salt the tripe, getting it into every crevice. Flip the tripe over and salt the smooth side, too. Place it in a bowl and add the vinegar, using an old toothbrush to scrub it all over.

Rinse the tripe, then place it in a pot and cover it with water. Bring to a boil and cook vigorously for 5 minutes. Remove the tripe and discard the water.

Put the tripe into a clean pot, then pour over enough water to cover. Add the star anise, bay leaves, cassia bark, Sichuan peppercorns, Shaoxing wine, scallions, and ginger. Simmer gently over low heat for 45 minutes.

Remove the tripe from the pot and reserve about 3½ tablespoons of the cooking liquid, discarding the rest. Place the tripe textured side down on a work surface and look carefully to see the direction of the grain. You want to cut rectangles about ¾ in (2 cm) wide and 2 in (5 cm) long with the grain going across the width of the strips. This will make it much more texturally pleasant to eat later.

Put the tripe pieces into a bowl with the cornstarch, satay sauce, chu hou paste, abalone sauce, salt, and sugar and massage it with your hands to get it into every nook and cranny. Leave for 10 minutes for the flavors to become friends. On a heatproof plate or bowl (that will fit inside a steamer), arrange the daikon batons in a rough mound and place the tripe, honeycomb side up, delicately in rows to cover the radish. Pour over any remaining sauce.

Prepare a bamboo steamer, then steam the tripe over high heat for 15–17 minutes until tender and the sauce is velvety. Garnish with slices of green and red chile and serve immediately.

Liusha Bao

Salted Egg Custard Buns
Makes 12 small buns

Liusha bao (流沙包) are an essential part of any dim sum. Every time I go to Hong Kong, I go to Lin Heung Tea House for dim sum. But, by the time of this book's publication, it will have closed down after 100 years of operation. I loved eating there, one of many hawk-eyed diners watching the trolley leave the kitchens, hoping to grab our favorite baskets before anyone else gets them.

The name for this bao literally translates as "quicksand bao." Its explosive ejaculation of salted duck egg filling is now known around the world thanks to social media, but it is adored by many because it is simply one of the most delicious bao ever. Long before there was salted caramel, there was salted duck egg custard.

6 salted egg yolks
10 tablespoons (150 g) unsalted butter, at room temperature
1⅓ cups (150 g) confectioners' sugar
¾ cup (75 g) dried milk powder
⅓ cup (75 ml) evaporated milk
1¾ oz (50 g) custard powder or cornstarch
1 x quantity Basic Baozi dough (see page 117)

Place the salted egg yolks in a small steamer over medium heat and steam for 10 minutes.

Beat together the butter and sugar in a bowl until creamy, then add the milk powder, evaporated milk, and custard powder or cornstarch and continue creaming until you have a smooth but firm paste.

Add the salted egg yolks and mash them into the paste until fully combined.

Divide the mixture into 12 equal-sized portions and roll them into balls. Place them in the fridge until ready to use. If your kitchen is very warm, put them into the freezer up to an hour.

Use the filling to make bao following the instructions on page 117, steaming them in paper cupcake or muffin cups.

It's important to make sure that these bao are firmly sealed, otherwise you will end up with filling everywhere.

Tang Soups

"Harmony may be illustrated by soup."

– Yen Tzu

In Confucianism, soup is a wonderful metaphor for the idea that harmony and agreement are not the same thing. We don't have to be unified in life or society to be harmonious. Like an orchestral symphony, a soup can have diverse parts that conflict without being violently opposed and which are balanced without being the same.

In China, there is no meal without soup, from the grandest dinner banquet to the most humble of breakfasts. Soups fill you up in a way that is inexpensive but still delicious. The cheapest cuts of meat with the most flavor are preferred, slow cooked to create clear and brilliant broths. Extracting the health benefits from meat, vegetables, and medicinal ingredients into a pure and palatable liquid is a process that can be traced back over 2,400 years.

In 2010, an archaeological dig near Xi'an discovered a sealed bronze pot containing the dried remnants of bone broth. Unfortunately, we don't have a recipe for this ancient soup, but we can start at the bottom end of the labor scale with a *mao tang* (毛汤), a simple blend of proteins that makes a frugal and flexible soup base. You will be given a small bowl of this broth to supplement many breakfasts in China. Sometimes it's a murky-looking dish with some scallions floating in it, at other times a deeper, richer *nong tang* (浓汤) that is fatty and clings to the palate.

The tradition of master stock, known as *lushui* (卤水), is of great interest, too. This is a broth that is kept simmering in perpetuity, with different ingredients added occasionally to impart their flavor. Some can be decades old and it is one of one of the prides of the Chinese kitchen. While not a soup you would drink or sip, various delicious toppings like *doufu jie* (豆腐结) or tofu knots (one of my absolute favorites) are cooked in it like flavor sponges, and a few extra spoons are often ladled over noodles for extra deliciousness.

Mao Tang 毛汤

Simple Broth
Makes 3–4 quarts (3–4 liters)

One of the building block recipes of Chinese cooking, this broth can be used either as a simple side dish to slurp, as the base of a bowl of soup noodles, or as an ingredient to poach delicate vegetables in for a spectacular banquet.

Often, the simplest recipes are the most contentious. Some will take a "less is more" approach, while others adapt and personalize with myriad unusual flavorings. But across all the provinces of China, the key pillars of making broth remain the same.

Any impurities are removed from the raw bones through a process of boiling and skimming or filtering. Primary additions always include ginger, to neutralize lingering odors rather than to add flavor. Other ingredients noted for their purifying properties include scallions, Shaoxing wine, or spices like Sichuan pepper.

Less common are sweetening ingredients, such as jujube (red dates), carrots, or corn. Some chefs will add a piece of salty ham from Jinhua or dried scallops, but this appears more in prestigious restaurants when making superior stock than in home cooking. I prefer to under-season my soup, instead adjusting the salt levels depending on the use.

The last common thread is the cooking time—always low and slow so as not to extract elements from the bones that would make the liquid cloudy.

This recipe will make a collagen-rich, almost creamy broth. If you want it less fatty, allow the broth to cool, then refrigerate it so that the jelly and fat separate. Remove the fat and the broth left behind will have a lighter and cleaner taste. The fat can be used to replace lard in any of the recipes in this book.

2 lb 4 oz (1 kg) pork bones or pork ribs
1 large chicken carcass (breasts, legs, thighs, and wings removed)
6 quarts (6 liters) water
1¾ oz (50 g) fresh root ginger, peeled and sliced
2–3 scallions (optional)

Put the pork and chicken into a large stockpot (at least 10-quart/10-liter capacity) and cover with water. Bring it to a boil, then after 10 minutes remove from the heat and discard the water.

Replenish the pot with the measured water and return the pot to the heat, this time over the lowest heat with the lid off. Add the ginger and scallions, if using.

After 30 minutes you will start to see white scum or foam floating on the surface. Gently remove it with a spoon or fine mesh strainer and discard. Check the broth every 30 minutes over the next 2 hours for impurities.

Cook for a total of 4 hours, during which time the broth will reduce by anything between 30 and 50 percent.

Remove from the heat and remove the bones with tongs. The meat can be separated from the bones and eaten with literally any sauce, noodle, or rice from this book. Remove the scallions and ginger and discard them.

Next, either ladle the broth through a sieve or pour it through a colander into a bowl to remove any small pieces. Leave the broth to cool to room temperature.

Portion the broth into containers or jars and chill in the fridge until it turns into a jelly.

It will keep in the fridge for 2 weeks or in the freezer for up to a year.

262

Zicai Danhuatang 紫菜蛋花汤

Egg Drop Soup

Serves 2

Fine, ghostly ribbons of egg floating in a simple broth, enriched with seaweed and served hot. It's a soup that is so ubiquitous that it can easily be overlooked. From my experience, this is not a dish that you request, it just arrives as part of an order, perhaps with a Lü Rou Huo Shao (see page 125) or a bowl of Re Gan Mian (see page 31). It's always there on the table, compliments of the chef. Whether you consume it or not is entirely up to you. It's part palate cleanser, with a delicate sea-saltiness that is hydrating and comforting. And for those with big appetites, it pushes you over the edge of contentment into fullness with only a scant number of calories.

If you have some of the simple broth opposite prepared, then preparation is low effort and high impact, turning a solitary breakfast dish into a feast.

⅛–¼ oz (5–7 g) dried seaweed (any type)
A large pinch of dried shrimp (optional)
Scant 1 cup (200 ml) water
Scant ½ cup (100 ml) Mao Tang (see opposite) or high-quality store-bought bone broth
1 egg, beaten
1 tablespoon sesame oil (optional)

263

Put the seaweed (and shrimp, if using) into a dry pot or wok and toast it lightly over medium heat for 3–4 minutes until fragrant.

Add the water and bring it to a gentle simmer, then add the broth and let it warm through.

Drizzle the beaten egg into the soup in a gentle stream, then gently stir the soup and almost immediately it is ready to serve.

Divide between two bowls and add a drizzle of sesame oil on top, if using.

花生汤

Huasheng Tang

Peanut Egg Drop Soup

Serves 4–6

Through the course of researching and writing this book, exploring the seemingly enormous diversity of Chinese morning meals, the rarest thing of all to come across was a completely sweet breakfast. From my observation, sugar is used in a similar way to salt, as a judicious seasoning. Indeed, the greatest compliment a Chinese person can make of any dessert is that it is "not too sweet."

That's why, on a visit to Quanzhou, a coastal culinary hub in southern Fujian province, I was pleasantly surprised to come across this breakfast/snack.

A light peanut soup, scalding hot, is poured over a beaten egg. On contact it scrambles, creating delicate ribbons. I always appreciate the contrast between the Western desire to create silky-smooth custards, terrified of scrambled eggs, and the Chinese approach that prizes them. In Lanzhou, I tried a similar dish made with hot milk, raisins, and sugar.

To accompany the dish was a selection of fried treats: regular *youtiao*, but also a sweetened variety and even one rolled in sugar like a Spanish churro. The most incredible side dish, however, was a deep-fried mashed taro cookie sandwich (see page 140).

4 cups (900 ml) water
⅓ cup (50 g) whole blanched peanuts
A pinch of salt
3–4 tablespoons smooth peanut butter
¼ cup (50 g) granulated sugar, or more to taste
2 eggs, beaten
Youtiao (see page 77) or other fried treats, to serve

Pour the water into a pot and bring to a boil, then add the peanuts and salt and cook for about 15 minutes until soft.

Add the peanut butter and whisk until it is fully incorporated. Add the sugar and bring the soup up to a rolling boil.

Ladle the scalding hot soup over the beaten eggs. It should immediately cook and curdle.

Enjoy straight away with fried treats on the side to dip and slurp.

Tianjiu Jidan

Sweet Rice Wine with Eggs
Serves 2

While researching this book, I spoke with my friend Joe Gong about his memories of growing up with his grandparents in Hunan for a year. His grandmother would prepare a simple homemade breakfast that resonates strongly with many Chinese of any age. It is *lao zao* (醪糟), a sweet fermented rice wine that goes by many other names depending on where you are from in China, with a poached egg and some brown sugar. She would add fresh *nian gao* (年糕) rice cakes that were cooked in the rice wine with a little water added.

How mysterious that this dish has not been picked up by street sellers or beautified for fancy restaurants, yet it encapsulates such a deep sense of shared family dining experience.

I absolutely adore lao zao; its delicate perfume, balanced sweetness, and simplicity make it a particularly good canvas for a morning meal. Its other magical use is to spoon a few tablespoons over vanilla ice cream.

Alongside this soup, Joe's grandmother would also serve a plate of Haozi Baba (see page 241), fried patties made with artemisia (aka wormwood), the same green herb used to make absinthe. They are popular across the southern Chinese provinces of Hunan and Guangxi, now often stuffed with sweet or savory fillings.

2 eggs
1½ oz (40 g) fresh rice cakes, often sold as "sliced rice cake" in an oval coin shape
1¼ cups (300 ml) lao zao (the type in a jar with pieces of rice floating in it)
Scant ½ cup (100 ml) water
Brown sugar, to serve (optional)

First poach the eggs to your preferred method, then set aside.

Cook the rice cakes according to the package instructions and set aside.

Pour the lao zao and water into a pot and bring to a gentle simmer. Add the cooked rice cakes and simmer gently for 3–4 minutes so they release a little starch into the soup.

Divide the rice wine and rice cakes between two bowls and add the poached eggs, then sweeten to your liking.

甜酒鸡蛋

Umaaqi

ئوماچ

Uyghur Corn Soup
Serves 3–4

While the Uyghur people of Xinjiang are known for their love of lamb and *nang* bread (see page 130), there is actually very little written about the rest of the culture's culinary landscape. In the provincial capital of Urumqi, however, I found restaurant after restaurant serving this velvety-smooth corn soup.

It's important to remember that the whole of China operates on one time zone: Beijing time. It's a bit like Los Angeles being on the same time as New York City. For the population out west, their day doesn't really start until 10 a.m.

I'm tempted to say that Campbell's cream of sweetcorn soup is very similar to this, but the thickening agent here is definitely starch and not dairy. The soup also contains enormous chunks of mutton bone that have been slow-cooked (separately from the corn soup) to stretch an otherwise low-cost soup. It was luck of the draw whether you had anything substantial worth gnawing on.

On the side was a Liangban Huang Luobo Si, with thin, long strands like noodles dressed in sharp vinegar with just a touch of chile (see page 288). This side salad is made in such a large quantity that it also becomes a default side for many lunch dishes.

Lastly, we had two types of steamed bun, one filled with a combination of beef meat and lamb fat, and the other, layered like an onion that fell apart into delicate pieces of dough (see page 110) that was dipped into a side dish of more vinegar and chile.

1 small onion, finely chopped
3¼ cups (500 g) corn kernels (fresh, canned, or frozen)
1⅔ cups (400 ml) water
Scant 1 cup (200 ml) lamb stock
1 teaspoon salt
½ teaspoon granulated sugar
1½ teaspoons cornstarch
3 tablespoons cold water
1–2 pieces of roasted lamb on the bone per person (optional)
Neutral oil, for frying

Heat a little oil in a pot over medium heat and gently fry the onion for 5–7 minutes until translucent but not browned.

Add the corn, water, lamb stock, salt, and sugar. Bring to a gentle simmer, then remove from the heat. Leave the soup to cool slightly for 10 minutes, then transfer to a blender or food processor and blend until smooth. You may need to do this in batches depending on the size of your blender. Return the soup to the pot.

Stir together the cornstarch with the cold water in a small bowl and add it to the soup.

Bring the soup to a simmer and cook for 30 minutes, stirring occasionally. It will thicken to a luscious, pourable soup.

Serve hot with the roast lamb pieces, if using.

Hu La Tang

胡辣汤

Barbarian Pepper Soup

Serves 2

This soup is a rich and fragrant soup from China's northern province of Henan. Both sour and extremely peppery, it's a wake-up dish that excites the senses. A single bowl, filled with vegetables, tofu skin, and a multitude of spices, will set you up for a long journey or almost any strenuous activity. Whether it's the incredibly thick consistency or the generous portion size, you're most certainly full for hours after a bowl of this soup. This recipe will also show you how to make *mianjin* (面筋) with flour, which splits the "muscle" of the gluten from the starch.

The name of the soup is particularly interesting. *La* (辣) means "spicy," but in this instance not from chile, and *tang* (汤) means "soup." But what about the first character? The word *hu* (胡) has a double meaning. In modern lingo, it is black pepper, and in this recipe, copious amounts of the stuff gives us fiery heat and piquancy. It was the main way to add heat before chile was introduced to China. But *hu* has another meaning, too. In around 500 BCE, it was used to describe barbarians, men with beards, or virtually anyone who wasn't culturally or ethnically Chinese. On the western borders during

this period, the powerful steppe kingdom of the Xiongnu (present-day Xinjiang) presented both a military threat and an alternative way of living. From just a simple dish, we can imagine Henan and Shaanxi as frontier provinces on the Silk Road, a region that was fought over both during the Warring States and the later Southern and Northern Dynasties period. The prefix "hu" can be found today in other words, such as walnuts (*hutao*, 胡桃) and the Chinese string instrument the *huqin* (胡琴), all introduced by those dashing barbarians with beards. Importantly, over the centuries of conflict, the fashion, interiors, music, and food of the Xiongnu people became fashionable within Chinese society, even with the elite and the emperor.

The first time I had this dish wasn't actually in Henan, but in Ningxia province. Ningxia has undergone considerable investment in the last few decades to transform it into China's burgeoning wine region. Today, Ningxia has a regional cuisine that is a combination of the tastes of its ancient sheep herder ancestors and those of its neighboring regions.

271

Hu La Tang

3⅓ cups (800 ml) water
A handful of raw peanuts, with skins
3½ oz (100 g) ground beef
¼ onion, diced, or 2 scallions (white parts
    only), chopped
⅓–½ oz (10–15 g) dried fine vermicelli noodles,
    broken into 1½ in (4 cm) pieces
1 thumb-sized piece of fresh root ginger,
    finely chopped
1 oz (30 g) dried day lily buds, cut into
    1½ in (4 cm) pieces
1 oz (30 g) dried wood ear mushrooms, cut in half
1 oz (30 g) fresh king oyster mushrooms
    (or shiitake)
1½ oz (40 g) dried yuba (tofu skins), cut into
    1½ in (4 cm) pieces
2–3 sheets dried seaweed (any type) or
    1 oz (30 g) fresh kelp, cut into 1½ in
    (4 cm) pieces
½ teaspoon Chinese five spice
½ teaspoon Chinese 13 spice
1 tablespoon freshly ground black pepper
1 tablespoon dark soy sauce
3½ tablespoons cold water
3½ tablespoons Zhenjiang vinegar
A few drops of sesame oil

For the mianjin
scant 1 cup (100 g) strong white bread flour
1⅔ cups (400 ml) water
A pinch of salt

272

The day before eating, prepare the mianjin. Combine the flour, ¼ cup (60 ml) of the water, and the salt in a bowl and knead together for 4–5 minutes to create a smooth ball of dough.

Put the dough into a large bowl and cover with the remaining water, then massage the dough in the water. This will release the starch from the dough into the water. After 15–20 minutes of massaging, you will be left with a stretchy piece of gluten dough and a bowl of milky starch water.

Remove the gluten dough, transfer to a separate bowl, cover, and refrigerate.

Cover the bowl of starch water and allow to sit overnight so that the wheat starch sinks to the bottom. Gently pour off the clear water, scrape the starch paste into a bowl, and cover. This wheat starch can also be used in place of the pea starch to make Liangfen (see page 63) or in place of cornstarch for thickening.

On the day of eating, prepare the soup. Combine the water and peanuts in a pot and bring to a boil to release the color from the peanuts, then reduce to a simmer.

Pull off as many small, thumb-sized pieces of gluten dough as you like and drop them into the water, then add the beef, onion, noodles, ginger, day lily, mushrooms, yuba, seaweed, five spice, 13 spice, black pepper, and soy sauce.

Mix 2 tablespoons of the wheat starch with the cold water. Add it to the soup, bring everything back up to a very gentle simmer, and stir as the soup thickens to the consistency of a thin custard.

Add the Zhenjiang vinegar and sesame oil and serve piping hot.

If you have any leftover mianjin, you can add a teaspoon of instant yeast to the dough and leave it to rise for 1 hour. Then steam the dough for 17–20 minutes and leave to cool before cutting it into chunky cubes. The interior will have the lightest crumb. Fry it with some soy sauce and sugar for a delicious topping for noodles.

Jingdezhen Rou Bing Tang

Jingdezhen
Meatball Soup
Serves 4–5

白如玉，明如镜，薄如纸，声如磬之称

"White like jade, bright as a mirror, thin as paper, and sounds like a bell."

A common breakfast in Jiangxi province, this soup is typically made in small brown terracotta pots with a thick rustic glaze, but in Jingdezhen they use the city's famous porcelain. They say that the porcelain of Jingdezhen is "white like jade, bright as a mirror, thin as paper, and sounds like a bell." With each serving cooked and served in individual porcelain bowls, the exquisiteness of almost 2,000 years of production has even trickled all the way down to breakfast.

Slow-simmered soups make up a key component of Jiangxi cuisine. The broth in this recipe is clear of impurities with a bright flavor that maintains the integrity of the ingredients. The individual bowls are prepared in a very large bamboo steamer, each with a meatball of pork that is flattened against the bowl. Topped with the clear soup, they go back into the steamer for 10 minutes until each is perfectly cooked. The soup is then finished with a liberal shake of white pepper and a spoonful of scallion.

I find it curious to see it made with this method, but there are obvious and perhaps less obvious reasons. One reason is that a large quantity of soup can be made slowly over many hours, but each customer has their individual breakfast cooked to order. This ensures that the broth remains pure while the meatball is poached to perfection. There is also a similar dish from Jiangxi called *wa guan tang* (瓦罐汤), or "crock pot soup,"

where individual pots of soup are sealed and stacked inside a primitive looking kiln. Considering the ceramic production of the province, the cooking techniques run parallel to its craft.

Steaming the porcelain bowl with the contents yields the biggest benefit; the soup stays scalding hot for almost the entire duration of the meal, perfect for chilly winter mornings.

9 oz (250 g) ground pork
1¾ oz (50 g) fresh root ginger, finely chopped
1 teaspoon finely ground white pepper, plus extra to serve
A pinch of salt
Enough Mao Tang to fill your serving bowls (see page 262)
Scallions (green parts only), finely chopped, to serve

Combine the pork, ginger, white pepper, and salt in a mixing bowl.

Form the mixture into balls and place one in each serving bowl. Flatten them with your hand into small patties so they will cook evenly.

Heat the broth in a small saucepan and prepare a bamboo steamer.

Pour the hot broth into the bowls, then place the bowls into the steamer. Steam over medium heat for 5–10 minutes until the meat is cooked through.

Serve with the scallion greens and an extra dash of white pepper.

274

景德镇肉饼汤

Paocai He Jiang Sauces and Pickles

Chinese sauces, pickles, ferments, and flavored waters are the building blocks of almost every dish.

I visited Ren Chang, one of the oldest soy sauce producers in Shaoxing, Zhejiang province, who have been producing soy sauce, *tianmianjiang* and vinegars for 11 generations. There, I learned how soy sauce was first developed, as a solution to the problem of an extraordinary glut of soy beans. This gradual repetition and trial and error created a product that, over many years, evolved from necessary innovation into tradition, heritage, and deeply rooted culture. What is so important in this story is that people had the time to experiment and, more importantly, fail in those experiments. It is a somewhat romantic idea that all of the delicious things in the world were usually discovered by accident by clumsy chefs and not through precise observation and skill. The owner of Ren Chang told me that their success is not just a legacy of human ingenuity, but also due to the fact that they are located in a very special Goldilocks zone for fermentation that stretches across China. Further north it is too cold and dry, further south too hot and humid. While fermentation is not impossible in less favorable conditions, it certainly has led to an abundance of products in Zhejiang.

What is so special about Ren Chang is their "mother and child" blend. Typically speaking, in Chinese soy sauce production, soy and wheat are mixed together and fermented. At Ren Chang, the wheat is steamed, fermented, and dried into bricks before being ground and added to the soy beans to make the new year's production. This step is the "child." That mixture is then blended with aged sauces from old vintages, also known as the "mother," creating a blend of years past that is also injected with a contemporary fermentation. The end product is a multi-faceted flavor profile that explores not only technique but also terroir.

There is enormous diversity and quality among small soy sauce producers, so I encourage you to seek out different brands and methods of production to add nuance and diversity to your meals. It can make all the difference. I remember a conversation I had with my friend, chef and artist Tongtong Ren, about her grandmother. Even when she was sick in bed, she would refuse to eat foods made with any other brands of soy sauce than the one she liked, sending it back to the kitchen for Tongtong's mother to remake.

If written recipes are a record of our cultural and culinary history, then pickles and ferments are living evidence of that legacy. They were born out of a need to survive or to deal with excess and abundance. To taste a soy sauce made with a mother that is over 300 years old is to taste history. With almost all Chinese breakfasts, vinegar or pickles take the meal from a simple piece of bread or plain noodles to another level.

Fuzhi Jiangyou

Infused Sichuan Soy Sauce

Makes 2 cups (500 ml)

复制酱油

If you've ever wondered why a simple dressing or sauce in a Chinese restaurant is exploding with flavor, yet when you make it at home it lacks a certain edge, then there are two reasons that you need to explore. Firstly, you could be avoiding MSG, the wonderful flavor crystals that can transform the flavor of everything from a Bolognese ragu to a martini. Or, secondly, you might be using soy sauce that is meant for cooking to finish or dress your dishes.

Fuzhi jiangyou (复制酱油) is an infused soy sauce, brewed with spices and sugar, which adds extra dimension and depth to your dishes. It is a fundamental part of Tianshui Mian (see page 24), which is an otherwise beginner-level noodle dish. Not only does it add flavor, it removes what can sometimes be described as an unpleasant bean flavor that soy sauce has when consumed straight. Make a batch and keep it in the fridge to use it to dress sesame noodles, poached chicken, or even Western-style salads.

2 pieces of cassia bark or 2 cinnamon sticks
3 star anise
4 bay leaves
6 cloves
10 black peppercorns
2 teaspoons Sichuan peppercorns
2 black cardamom pods
2 teaspoons fennel seeds
⅓ oz (10 g) dried orange peel
1 cup (250 ml) dark soy sauce
1 cup (250 ml) light soy sauce
Scant ½ cup (100 ml) water
1¾ oz (50 g) rock sugar
4 scallions
2 thumb-sized pieces of fresh root ginger
3–4 garlic cloves, peeled

Put the dried spices and orange peel into a heatproof bowl and cover with boiling water. Set aside to soak for 1 minute. This is similar to soaking and discarding the first infusion of oolong tea. The idea is to take away any dust or acrid flavor but also to make the dried spices more supple and ready for infusion.

Strain the spices and add them to a pot with the remaining ingredients.

Bring the mixture to a gentle boil and cook for 30 minutes until glossy, then remove from the heat. Cover with a lid and set aside to infuse until completely cool.

Strain the mixture through a fine sieve into an airtight container or jar and store in the fridge for up to 2 months.

Lao Lijiang Lazi Jiang

老丽江辣子酱

Lijiang Chile Paste
Makes 12 oz (350 g)

In the old town market of Lijiang, Yunnan, is an entrepreneurial duo that has set up a chile paste stand. As opposed to the chile crisp that has become enormously trendy in the last few years, which is a simple oil infusion, this is more akin to a pesto in texture, using walnuts and peanuts as the base. I once took a kilo tub of it to Miao Lu (see page 70), and they loved it so much that it has become something of a talking point and now appears on the table throughout the day. We would spread it on corn cakes from the market and drizzle them with local honey.

At the market, the couple grind a simple array of ingredients into a rough paste using a food processor and then pass it through what looks like a meat grinder attached to a small motor engine. The finished result is a condiment that can be used for cooking and for eating like a dip or spread. Thick and homogeneous, it has an incredible intensity of flavor.

While the ingredients the pair use are on show, the all-important ratios are less obvious. This recipe is my approximation, following some trial and error testing.

If you can't find dried Barbarian chile, you can substitute another kind. You just need two types of chile—one that is smooth and mellow with a smoky and fruity taste like Pasilla de Oaxaca or Pequin, and another to provide a kick of heat.

1¾ oz (50 g) dried Barbarian chiles (胡辣椒)
1¾ oz (50 g) dried bird's eye chiles
1⅔ tablespoons Sichuan peppercorns
1¾ cups (200 g) walnut halves
⅓ cup (50 g) white sesame seeds
⅔ cup (100 g) whole blanched peanuts
1¾ oz (50 g) toasted soy bean flour
   (often sold as kinako)
4 teaspoons sesame oil, plus extra to store
4 teaspoons peanut oil

Put the chiles into a food processor and process them into small pieces about the size of a chile seed or grain of rice.

Add the rest of the ingredients and process on medium speed for 7–10 minutes, scraping down the sides occasionally, until you have a spreadable chile paste consistency. As the walnuts, peanuts, and sesame seeds start to break down they will release their oils and this will create the paste so be patient.

Decant into a jar, then top with a layer of oil as an airlock to prevent it from going bad. Store in the fridge and consume within two weeks.

279

Sauces and Pickles

Lazi Jiang

Chile Crisp

Makes about 6⅓ cups (1.5 liters)

My good friend Jing Gao, creator of Fly By Jing, the poster child for new-wave chile sauces, once said to me: "MSG is a crutch." At one point in history, it was a tool of flavor democratization—everyone, regardless of income, could enjoy delicious, appetizing foods. After the Second World War, it was almost necessary to bridge the gap. I have absolutely no problem with it and use it myself, but I do sometimes feel that its use is more habitual than useful. Fortunately, we don't live in that world anymore, and where possible, we can source high-quality ingredients that provide flavor without the use of this enhancer.

I was with Jing in Chengdu as we decided to do some filming for her (at that time) new company. We spent the day in a rented apartment with a beautiful kitchen, making batches of her now world-famous chile crisp as well as several hundred different colored dumplings. I observed how careful the layering of flavors was and how nuanced her palate was even after eating spoon after spoon of blisteringly hot chile crisp.

The next day, we took a car and drove for hours into the mountains west of Chengdu. In the remote foothills at the start of the Silk Road on the way to Myanmar we stopped to

pick *gongjiao* (贡椒), or "tribute pepper," a special variety of Sichuan peppercorn that was once so highly prized it was only grown for the emperor. It's practically impossible to find this chile elsewhere in China.

Today, chile crisp has become incredibly well-known outside of China, being used on everything from scrambled eggs to soft-serve ice cream. While the original brand is and will always be Lao Gan Ma (that disgruntled old woman who became a multi-billionaire off the back of chile oil), it was Jing who created the mindset that something produced in China could be well-crafted and high-quality, made without the use of shortcuts or crutches. Her recipe uses a mixture of three common Chinese chiles: *xiao mi la* (小米辣), *er jing tiao* (二荆条), and *hong deng long* (红灯笼). Their purpose is to create a complex spice profile that is sweet, aromatic, and smoky. I once made a version of this sauce with seven varieties of dried Mexican chiles and dubbed it "Mexi-chuan"—for me, part of the joy of making homemade chile crisp is the experimentation. If you can't find the chiles Jing uses, feel free to try a different combination—the most important thing is to use a variety to ensure a multi-dimensional sauce.

4–5 dried shiitake or chestnut mushrooms
1¾ oz (50 g) dried xiao mi la chiles
1¾ oz (50 g) dried er jing tiao chiles
1¾ oz (50 g) dried hong deng long chiles
4¼ cups (1 liter) neutral oil
2 star anise
1 large piece of cassia bark
2–3 Chinese white cardamom pods (don't
    substitute green cardamom here)
3–4 large slices of fresh root ginger
2 shallots, thinly sliced
4–5 garlic cloves, sliced
1 tablespoon granulated sugar
2 tablespoons doubanjiang (chilli bean paste) or
    2 tablespoons of douchi (whole fermented
    black beans), roughly chopped
2 tablespoons Sichuan peppercorns (ideally red)

Put the mushrooms into a food processor and
blend to a fine powder, then remove and set aside.
(Alternatively, you can buy mushroom powder
from specialist stores online.)

Put the chiles into the food processor and blend
them into fine pieces, but not into a powder. You
are looking for small chunks the size of sesame
seeds or rice.

Heat the oil in a pot over medium heat until small
bubbles start to form on the bottom of the pot.
If you place a wooden chopstick or spoon into
the oil and it gently sizzles, the oil is at the right
temperature.

Add the star anise, cassia bark, cardamom pods,
and slices of ginger and gently infuse them for
5 minutes. Keep an eye on the temperature and
reduce it if necessary. You don't want the items to
burn, but rather to infuse the oil.

Remove the spices from the oil with a slotted
spoon and discard them. At this point the oil might
be gently smoking, but this is OK.

283

Remove the oil from the heat and leave it for a
minute to cool slightly, then gently sprinkle in the
ground chiles. If you throw it all in one go, there's
a chance it will erupt and overflow—a serious
hazard, so take it easy.

Once the chile has been added, add the shallots,
garlic, sugar, doubanjiang or douchi, mushroom
powder, and the Sichuan peppercorns. The reason
we add the Sichuan pepper at the end is that it
burns easily and can give a strong acrid flavor.

Leave the chile crisp to cool completely in the pot,
then pour into glass jars. Store in a cool, dark place
for a few days, or ideally a week, to let the flavors
mellow and integrate. Keep it in a cool dark place
and it will last for a very long time, although you will
probably eat it all within a week.

Serve on everything—yes, everything.

Sichuan Fengwei Mala Luobo Gan

Sichuan-Style Ma La Dried Daikon Pickle

Makes 14 oz–1 lb 2 oz (400–500 g)

四川风味麻辣萝卜干

This is a pressed radish pickle that adds so much to so many dishes. It is typically served in Sichuan with Douhua (see page 195) or as a side dish to many of the province's dumpling dishes. It is low effort to prepare but does take some advanced planning.

The *baijiu* (an incredibly strong Chinese grain spirit) plays the role of sterilizing and keeping the pickles fresh for up to a year with proper storage. I add these pickles to scrambled eggs or even use them in sandwiches for a crunch with a punch.

284

1 lb 2 oz (500 g) daikon, peeled and cut into
   1 x 1½ in (4 cm) batons
1 tablespoon salt, plus 1 teaspoon for the
   marinade
2 teaspoons granulated sugar
1 tablespoon chile powder or ground chile flakes
5 tablespoons chile oil
2 teaspoons ground Sichuan pepper
1 teaspoon Chinese five spice
½ teaspoon MSG
3 tablespoons baijiu, or vodka at a pinch
2 teaspoons toasted white sesame seeds

Put the daikon into a bowl and sprinkle over the salt, then mix well. Set aside for 3–4 hours to extract as much water as possible. Wash the salt off and dry the daikon with a tea towel.

Place the daikon on a piece of cheesecloth and close it up into a pouch. Place it in a colander that fits into a large bowl and place a pan on top, then fill the pan with as many cans or other heavy objects as you can. Press the daikon for 2 days, discarding the water in the bowl every 8–12 hours.

To sterilize your jars, wash them thoroughly with soap, rinse well, then place them in a large pot with the lids (and rubber seals). Submerge them in boiling water and boil vigorously for 10 minutes. Allow them to cool completely before handling and don't touch the inside of the jar.

Remove the daikon from the cheesecloth and dry it thoroughly with paper towels or a tea towel, then transfer to a large bowl.

Stir together the remaining salt for the marinade with all the other ingredients and add to the daikon. Massage the marinade into the daikon so that every piece is coated.

Pack the daikon into sterilized jars and store them in a cool, dark place for up to a year.

Sichuan Pao Cai

Sichuan Pickles
Makes about 2 lb 4 oz (1 kg) pickles

There are two main categories of pickles and preserves in Chinese culture: those that are marinated, like the Sichuan daikon pickle opposite, and those that are fermented in a brine, which use the help of lactic bacteria to create sourness, like this one.

For this recipe, you should invest in a traditional Chinese pickle jar. If you love pickling then they're an excellent investment. They look like a glass vase with a collar around the neck and a glass lid. The collar is where you add water to create an airlock, a concept also used in Korean-style *ongi*. The key difference is that the glass gives you the ability to see if things are going wrong and correct them before it's too late. If you see any mold growing on the jar, dip a tissue in some alcohol and wipe it clean.

If you are going on vacation, top up the water seal to the top and cover the jar with a loose-fitting plastic bag to slow down the evaporation. Never let the water seal dry out otherwise your pickles will go bad quickly.

In this process there is no need to pre-salt or cook the vegetables, just make sure they are clean and thoroughly dried. Focus on vegetables with crunch like carrots, parsnips, peas in the pod, cabbage, broccoli, and whole chile peppers, as well as aromatic herbs like bay leaves, cilantro, and parsley. White cabbage and chile is a popular combination.

Enjoy these with a bowl of dumplings or noodles, or finely shred them and use them as a filling for toasted Baozi (see page 115).

5 quarts (5 liters) water
30–40 Sichuan peppercorns
¾ cup (250 g) salt
10 dried xiao mi la or bird's eye chiles, dried
1 bulb of garlic, cloves peeled
4 large slices of fresh root ginger
1¾ oz (50 g) cilantro or parsley leaves
1 white cabbage, leaves separated and cut into halves or thirds
½ daikon or 10–15 radishes, cut into bite-sized pieces or batons
1 lb 2 oz (500 g) cowpeas, green beans, or long beans, left whole
1 celtuce root or ½ cauliflower, cut into bite-sized pieces or batons
1¾ oz (50 g) rock sugar
Scant ½ cup (100 ml) baijiu or high-alcohol vodka (around 60 percent proof)

First, prepare your pickle jar by sterilizing it (see opposite).

Pour the water into a pot and bring to a boil, then remove from the heat and add the Sichuan peppercorns and salt. Stir until the salt has completely dissolved. Once it has cooled, pour the brine into the pickle jar.

Put the chiles, garlic, ginger, and herbs into the jar, then artfully arrange the vegetables in layers.

Add the rock sugar to the top of the pickle brine and top it up with the baijiu so that everything is completely covered by liquid.

Add a little water to the moat of the jar, then add the lid. Top up the water moat and store the jar in a cool and dark place. On day 14, test the pickles for contamination—strong musty flavors will be the giveaway. It should taste salty and sour. If it has gone bad, discard it and start again.

At around 21–28 days, your vegetables should be ready to consume and at this stage it's best to remove all the solid elements from the brine. Remove between one quarter and one fifth of the liquid, too, and replace it with new water, baijiu, sugar, and spices. Over time, your pickle brine will deepen in flavor and every batch you produce will be more delicious.

凉拌紫甘蓝

Liangban Ziganlan

Purple Cabbage Salad
Serves 4–6

There is a terrible stereotype that the Chinese do not eat salads. In all my time visiting and living in China I found an incredible diversity of fresh, crisp, and balanced cold raw vegetable plates that accompany mostly fatty, meaty, or spicy dishes.

One of my favorite Chinese salads (which is sadly not served at breakfast) is from Hunan. It is made with unripe pear that is cut into long matchsticks and scallions, and is dressed with rice vinegar and sesame oil. As a side dish for barbecued meats it's utterly explosive and I recommend it for any summer lunch or dinner.

This particular salad was served to me alongside a bowl of Lanzhou's famous pulled noodles (see page 39). It was one of the recurring side dishes that every restaurant in Lanzhou I visited prepared as part of their *xiao cai* (小菜), or small vegetable plates, which also usually included very tart pickled radishes. In Xinjiang, these same dishes were described as *liang cai* (凉菜), cold dishes to go with meaty mains and spicy soups.

The benefit of this recipe is that it doesn't require any special knowledge of pickling and can be made a few hours ahead of serving.

½ red cabbage, shredded
2 teaspoons salt
1 tablespoon granulated sugar
⅓ cup (75 ml) rice vinegar
½ teaspoon ground white pepper
1 tablespoon sesame oil
1 tablespoon toasted white sesame seeds
1 oz (30 g) cilantro, leaves picked

287

Put the cabbage into a bowl, add the salt, and massage it into the cabbage for 1 minute. Cover and chill in the fridge for 1 hour.

Meanwhile, combine the rest of the ingredients in a bowl and set aside.

Remove the cabbage from the fridge and drain off any liquid but don't wash off the salt. Add the dressing and give it a second massage. Refrigerate again for 30 minutes, then serve with something hot and spicy.

Liangban Huang Luobo Si

سوغاق سەي

Uyghur Carrot Slaw
Serves 4–6

During my time in Xinjiang, there wasn't a Uyghur restaurant that didn't have a large bowl of carrot salad somewhere for customers to help themselves to. After reading many recipes for this dish I felt there was a tendency to doll it up far more than what was truly on offer in Turpan, Urumqi, or Kashgar.

Keep in mind that the carrots in Xinjiang are enormous compared to their Western supermarket counterparts. They have a much more intense sweetness and color, too—bordering on a blood orange in intensity. I recommend buying the best-quality heritage variety carrots you can find. The vinegar used in Xinjiang was sharp and directional, more like distilled vinegar than something rounded like white wine vinegar or apple cider vinegar. It was combined with just a shadow of chile. Something from Kashmir is ideal here, as it has more of a fruity depth than just raw heat.

Lastly, if you were one of those who invested in a spiralizer or have a handy julienne peeler, they work far better than a box grater, creating long and thin noodle strands.

2–3 large carrots, finely spiralized or julienned
2 tablespoons salt
3½ tablespoons distilled white vinegar
2 teaspoons Kashmiri chile powder

Put the carrots into a bowl, add the salt, and gently massage it into the carrots for 1 minute. Cover and set aside for 30 minutes.

Thoroughly rinse the carrots, then dry completely with paper towels or a tea towel.

In a clean bowl, combine the carrots with the vinegar and chile powder and massage again for 1 minute.

Cover and refrigerate. It will be ready to eat in 1 hour but will happily last for 2 days and will get better over time.

凉拌黄萝卜丝

Glossary

Artemisia (*aiye*, 艾叶)
Also known as silvery wormwood or Chinese mugwort, *Artemisia argyi* is a popular plant in traditional Chinese medicine. It is tart, bitter, and strongly aromatic, with a flavor that's like a mixture of mint, juniper, and sage. The *Artemisia* genus also includes *A. vulgaris*, *A. absinthium* and *A. annua*, which all have various medical or culinary uses across the world.

Baijiu (白酒)
China's national alcohol, this is a strong, colorless distilled spirit made from sorghum, but other grains can be added too. It can be anything from 40 to 80 percent proof. The most famous brand, Maotai, can fetch hundreds of thousands of dollars per bottle.

Cardamom, black (*cao guo*, 草果)
A larger pod than either of its cousins, black cardamom has as a smoky flavor with a similar flavor profile to green cardamom, although less intense. If used as part of a blend of spices, it's OK to leave it out.

Cardamom, white (*bai dou kou*, 白豆蔻)
White cardamom has a gentle minty citrus flavor. It is mostly used whole and layered with other spices. If you can't find it, it's OK to leave it out.

Cassia bark (*gui pi*, 桂皮)
Also known as Chinese cinnamon, this dried tree bark is less pungent that the true cinnamon you will be familiar with. Use it in savory dishes to create richness in the same way that bay leaves do. You can substitute it for cinnamon sticks, just use less.

290

Century eggs (*pi dan*, 皮蛋)
These eggs are preserved in a mixture of quick lime, clay, ash, salt, and rice for several weeks or months until they are chemically cured. The texture is soft and creamy with a delicate flavor. Stir them into congee for breakfast or eat them with silken tofu and a spicy dressing.

Chiles (*lajiao*, 辣椒)
Fresh or dried, there are hundreds of varieties of chile now unique to Chinese cooking. However, for all Chinese varieties, there is an equivalent within Mexican or Caribbean cooking in terms of flavor profile and Scoville-scale intensity.

In Chinese recipes, if there is no description of what type of chile is used, it is most likely *chao tian jiao* (朝天椒), or facing heaven chile, which is remarkably easy to grow at home. These chiles offer a wide range of heat, from 10,000 to 50,000 Scoville Heat Units (SHU), similar to tabasco, cayenne, or serrano chiles.

Other varieties used in this book include *hu la jiao* (胡辣椒), or Barbarian chile, which has the intensity of heat of a facing heaven chile but with the delicious sweetness of a bell pepper. It also has a smoky flavor from the drying process. The *xiao mi la* (小米辣) chile pepper has a more intense heat (around 75,000 SHU), similar to a bird's eye chile. *Er jing tiao* (二荆条), sometimes referred to as the Sichuan long chile, has a characteristic curved shape with a milder background heat. Lastly, *hong deng long* (红灯笼), known as red lanterns, are round and bright red with a medium spice level. They are often cooked whole in dishes. Using high-quality red lanterns to make chile oil will ensure it has a lovely red brightness rather than a muddy brown color.

When substituting chile varieties, I feel there are two approaches. You can either use a single type of chile and focus on the purity of flavor, adjusting quantity to control intensity. Or you can create a blend, taking into consideration spiciness, aroma, smokiness, and sweetness to create a balance.

Chinese five spice (*wu xiang fen*, 五香粉)
The standard spice mix of star anise, cloves, cassia bark, Sichuan pepper, and fennel seeds.

Chinese 13 spice (*shi san xiang*, 十三香)
This spice mix uses the base of five spice (see above) with an additional eight ingredients: black pepper, nutmeg, white peony, orange peel, angelica root, liquorice, galangal, and *Wurfbainia villosa*, known as *sharen* (砂仁), which is a relative of ginger. You'll recognize it from its small brown and yellow box with a rather disgruntled man on it.

Dried day lily flowers (*huang hua*, 黄花)
These are the dried unopened buds of day lily flowers. They add extraordinary flavor and meatiness to vegetarian dishes.

Doubanjiang 豆瓣酱
A thick sauce made from fermented fava beans, this is a fundamental ingredient in Sichuan cuisine, with amazing versatility from cooking to dipping sauces. One of the most popular varieties is from Pixian (a district of Chengdu now called Pidu), so look out for the name. Examples from this district can be fermented for up to three years to develop deep, funky complexity. A jar will keep forever in the fridge.

Douchi (豆豉)
These fermented and salted black beans are used to add complexity to strongly flavored dishes. They have a funky aroma that mellows with cooking. You could also sub for *doubanjiang* (see above).

Furu (腐乳)
Fermented tofu in a jar, there are thousands of brands all producing different styles. It is often called "Chinese cheese" due to its creamy, spreadable texture and funky, almost blue-cheese aroma. Yunnan-style *furu* in chile is my favorite for breakfast and is widely available. Other styles include Fujian-style, which is packed in red yeast and which gives *char siu* pork its characteristic flavor, and Changzhou-style, which is packed in sweet rice wine and has a gentler, Cheddar cheese flavor.

291

Garlic chives (*jiucai*, 韭菜)
These are like long, flat scallions with a strong aroma and flavor of garlic. Substitute with the green part of scallions and raw garlic or, if in season, wild garlic.

Glutinous rice (*nuomi*, 糯米)
Also known as sticky or sweet rice, this is common across Asia for its unique characteristics if cooked properly. It is used whole in several dishes in this book such as Ci Fan Tuan (see page 158) and Lawei Nuomi Fan (see page 170) to name a few. In its ground form it is used to make desserts such as *tangyuan* (汤圆; glutinous rice balls served in sweet soup) and rice cakes.

Gypsum (*shigao*, 石膏)
Gypsum is the alkalizing mineral used for tofu production. It can be bought online in powdered or solid form and may be listed as calcium sulfate. Make sure to buy pure, food-grade gypsum.

Jujube (*hongzao*, 红枣)
Also known as Chinese or red dates, these are a dried or candied fruit used in cooking but which are also a great snack with tea or coffee. In their raw, fresh state they taste like a crisp apple. Look out for *gou tou zao* (狗头枣) that taste like marshmallow.

Lap cheong (臘腸)
A popular dried Cantonese sausage made with pork and sometimes liver.

Lao zao (醪糟)
A partially fermented sweet and aromatic rice wine. It is used both in breakfast and dessert recipes. It is the first stage of fermentation and as such is typically less than 1 percent alcohol. It is easy to make at home with rice yeast but can be bought in most Chinese supermarkets in large jars.

Glossary

Lye water (*jian shui*, 枧水)

This alkaline solution is an acidic regulator used in baking. It creates a distinctive chewy texture for noodles and things like bagels. It also adds a deep golden color after baking. Use this in precise amounts, though, or there will be an unpleasant aftertaste.

Mi jiu (米酒)

Mi jiu refers to wine fermented from rice and, depending on context, style of production, or province, can be anything from 10 to 50 percent alcohol. All cooking wines, such as those from Shaoxing (see below), come under this category, as well as the Sichuan homemade moonshine called *changjiu* (常酒). In cooking it has two main uses: either to neutralize or to enhance strong flavors.

Millet (*xiaomi*, 小米)

This tiny yellow cereal is eaten mostly as a porridge. Not to be confused with the electronics company of the same name.

Oil (*you*, 油)

A neutral oil with a high smoking point will do wonders for your cooking. While sunflower, vegetable, and peanut are all perfectly fine, many Chinese cooks use pure canola oil (*cai you*, 菜油). It offers one of the best quality-to-price ratios and is my personal choice for the Chile Crisp on page 282.

Orange peel (*chenpi*, 陈皮)

These whole dried mandarin peels are used in sweet and savory cooking, infused in tea, and are a key ingredient in traditional Chinese medicine. They have a prominent sweet taste with a strong bitter aftertaste. Available in all Asian supermarkets, but easy to make at home, too.

Sand ginger (*shajiang*, 沙姜)

Also known as greater galangal or aromatic ginger, it is similar to its more common relative but with a more pronounced pepperiness. Combine ground ginger and white pepper to make a suitable substitute.

292 **Sesame paste (*zhimajiang*, 芝麻酱)**

A dark brown sesame paste similar to tahini. The seeds are toasted before grinding, which gives the paste an intense color and removes any unwanted bitterness. Pair it with a wei shui (see opposite) to make a delicious sauce for noodles.

Shang jin (上劲)

A method for whipping meat with great vigor and gusto in order to emulsify proteins. Most chefs will use their hand in the shape of a claw and beat the mixture in one direction, combining it with any other ingredients. This technique ensures that the fillings for recipes like Siu Mai (see page 248) and Xiao Jiaozi (see page 217) are juicy rather than soggy.

Shaoxing wine (绍兴酒)

A particular style of *huangjiu* (黄酒), or yellow wine. To make sure you're buying a quality product, look for *huadiao* (花雕) on the bottle, as this is one of the highest grades. A good-quality sherry works as a subsitute.

Shepherd's purse (*jicai*, 荠菜)

Part of the mustard family, this leafy vegetable has a strong peppery flavor. The leaves are best when young and can be eaten raw, too. Nowadays this can be commonly found in Asian supermarkets in the freezer section.

Sichuan pepper (*hua jiao*, 花椒) and Sichuan pepper oil (*hua jiao you*, 花椒油)

The iconic numbing flavor of central Chinese cuisine comes from this tiny citrus fruit. It is best to buy the peppercorns whole and remove the black seed in the middle before cooking or grinding. The pressed oil should be a delicate green color and is great for finishing dishes.

Snow fungus (*yin er*, 银耳)

Literally "silver ear" in Mandarin, this mushroom (*Tremella fuciformis*) is also known as snow ear or white wood ear. On its own it's tasteless, but it is prized for its gelatinous texture and health properties. It is used almost exclusively in sweet dishes and can also be found in beautifying health drinks.

Glossary

Soy sauce (*jiang you*,酱油)

Soy sauce is split into two categories, light, and dark, which are known in China as young (*sheng*, 生) and old (*lao*, 老). Light soy sauce is saltier, with a robust taste and is used in general cooking, marinades, and dipping sauces. Dark soy sauce is rich and glossy and is used primarily for color. In China, soy sauce is graded by the level of amino acids rather than by style or production techniques. "Special grade" is 0.8 mg (or greater) per 3½ fl oz (100 ml), "first grade" is 0.7 mg, "second grade" is 0.55 mg, and "third grade" is 0.4 mg, but either way you should always try to buy soy sauce that is naturally fermented.

The majority of soy sauce uses wheat in their production, but if you are looking for a gluten-free option, some producers make soy sauce with only fermented beans. Alternatives are Japanese tamari or coconut aminos from the health food aisle.

Suan cai (酸菜)

These are salted and fermented Chinese mustard greens (*jie cai*, 芥菜). You can make them at home using the Sichuan Pao Cai recipe from page 285 and omitting the alcohol, otherwise you can easily find them in Asian supermarkets either in jars or vacuum-packed pouches. The leaves are finely chopped and added to many dishes but they are often cooked with pork to cut through the meat's fattiness.

Tianmianjiang (甜面酱)

Literally "sweet flour sauce," this is made from fermented wheat and is typically used in northern China. It is the sauce that accompanies Peking duck and is the smear of sauce on a jianbing. It is widely available, but if you can't find it, some doubanjiang (see page 291) mixed with a touch of sugar will work in its place.

Vinegars (*cu*, 醋)

There are four main categories of vinegar in China and, unlike Western vinegars, they are produced from grains rather than grapes. Sichuan's Baoning vinegar is more savory than sweet and is essential for Sichuan cooking. Jiangsu's Zhenjiang (or Chinkiang) black vinegar is a common table condiment, mildly acidic and sweeter than Baoning. They are both widely available in the West.

The other two are less common or can only be found online. Shanxi's aged sorghum-based mature vinegar (*chen cu*, 陈醋) has a thicker consistency and incredible complexity, making it perfect for rich meats like lamb. If you can't find it, use Zhenjiang and add some liquid smoke. Fujian's red yeast rice vinegar is most popular in southern coastal areas—its low acidity works well with seafood. A substitute would be balsamic vinegar mixed with some ground black sesame seeds.

Wei shui (味水)

These "flavor waters" are infusions of spices and herbs that can be used to thin sauces, deglaze pans, or add complexity to braised dishes. They are a great way to add subtle flavor but can also be used to control volatile flavors and balance a dish.

Zhacai (榨菜)

The fermented swollen stem of the mustard plant, it can be plainly salted or coated in chile paste. It is usually sold whole or in batons. It is the pickle of choice for Dan Dan Mian (see page 36) and in Ci Fan Tuan (see page 158).

Zhe er gen (折耳根)

Known as fish mint or chameleon plant, this rhizome root is used particularly in southern Chinese and South East Asian cooking and has a particular combination of fishy and menthol flavors. Serve it as a salad or make it into spicy relish to go with the meat pies on page 90.

293

Index

295

Index

Index

297

Index

299

Index

Vegan, Vegetarian, and Gluten-Free Recipes

300

Cook's Notes

All fruits and vegetables are assumed to be medium-sized and washed.
Garlic, onions, and ginger are assumed to be peeled.
Herbs are assumed to be fresh unless stated otherwise.
All eggs are large.
Salt is fine table salt unless stated otherwise.
Sugar is white granulated sugar unless stated otherwise.

Acknowledgments

Thank you to my greatest support, my husband, Mark. Without your ability to fearlessly explore the unknown and your willingness to go on any adventure, this wouldn't have been possible. The spark to get this book written has come from you.

To my parents, Peter and Yvonne, the most wonderful parents I could ask for. Persistence and hard work are just two of the things I have learned from you. Thanks also to my sister, Natalie—our first trip to China all those years ago opened my eyes to a world beyond our childhood—and my hilarious brothers, Paul and Martin.

To my Chinese family: my cousin, Beili, my late uncle, Hexie, and my auntie, Lizhu. I owe my love and gratitude to the entire Xu family that hosted me on the many visits to Zhoushan Island over the years.

My Auntie Pauline and Uncle Robin: thank you for the meticulous records about granddad and his voyages across the world. I can only say I wish I had known him longer.

To Alex Xu and Cadence Hardenbergh, for the countless conversations and bottles of wine, for your knowledge and patience. Thanks to the entire team at Miao Lu for their generosity and skill. I can't wait to celebrate with you all.

DJ Zhang, you salty dog. We know who is number one. Betty Richardson, my original trog wife—I will treasure our early travels to far-flung restaurants in the middle of nowhere. From you I really learned that anything is possible in a Didi Premier.

Jamie Peñaloza, I am thankful for your endless desire to taste and see everything. Our travels through Sichuan, Gansu, and Guangdong have enriched this experience so much. You are both an ardent learner and accomplished master of your craft.

Thank you to Atina Kuo, and your father, auntie, and brother, for guiding me through not only Xinjiang but also the life and culture of the Xibo people. I hope you get that documentary made soon.

Hongwei Dai: for years you have been my guide through Chinese subcultures, countless obscure markets, and dishes from generations past. Many of the recipes are here because of you.

Peiran Gong and Tongtong Ren from Chinese Laundry, your insights and perspective on family, flavor, and memory through the medium of food have greatly impacted me and this book. Food is emotion, both pleasure and pain, that comes to bear on us all.

Maryam and Philippe, my Shanghai mother and father, thank you for all the martinis and the dancing, shelter, and love.

Francesca Tarocco, my *shifu*, thank you for guiding me and (more often) correcting me, too.

To my friends Denis Sdobnov, Crystyl Mo, Henrietta Lovell, Brian Garcia, Joe Gong, Johnson Chuang, Scott Wong, Lexie Comstock, Cat Nelson, Jacky Chan, and Cathy Chon. Thank you for everything, from a bowl of noodles and a friend on the road to a night on the sofa or a bag of cookies.

Thanks to Denis and Jacqueline and the entire team of The Middle House in Shanghai, The Opposite House in Beijing, and The Temple House in Chengdu. Also to Brian and Jeanee Linden and the team of the Linden center in Xizhou.

Jenny Lau, thank you for all your help and guidance—hopefully I'll find out where I'm really from someday. Thanks to Wei Guo for your incredible encouragement and championing of this project.

Thank you to my absolutely divine agent, Cathryn Summerhayes, and to the dream team who brought this book together: my editors, Kitty Stogdon and Lucy Kingett, who made sense of my nonsense, and to Christopher O'Leary for the design that has gone so far beyond my wildest expectations—it is a beauty!

And lastly, thank you to all cooks and chefs of all the breakfasts in every corner, village, and kitchen of China I visited. Thank you from the bottom of my heart for feeding and nurturing this book.

Michael Zee is the creator of the online sensation SymmetryBreakfast, which has been featured in newspapers and magazines including the *Guardian*, *Washington Post,* and *Telegraph* among many others. His British-Chinese heritage, including growing up helping out in his parents' Chinese restaurants and five years spent living in Shanghai, means he is uniquely placed to document the huge variety of Chinese breakfast foods. His aim is to break down the barriers to Chinese cooking by developing recipes that are as accessible as possible. *Zao Fan: Breakfast of China* is his third book after *Cook Love Share* (2016) and *Eat Like a Local SHANGHAI* (2019). A lifelong wandering soul, he is currently based in Rome, Italy, following stints in London and Bologna.

First published in 2024 by

Interlink Books
An imprint of Interlink Publishing Group, Inc.
46 Crosby Street
Northampton, Massachusetts 01060
www.interlinkbooks.com

Published simultaneously in the UK by Bloomsbury Publishing Plc.

A note on the pinyin: every effort has been made to transliterate accurately. Where variations exist, the most common iteration has been used

Library of Congress Cataloging-in-Publication Data available
ISBN 978-1-62371-695-0

10 9 8 7 6 5 4 3 2 1

Project Editor: Lucy Kingett
American Edition Editor: Leyla Moushabeck
Designer: Chris O'Leary
Photographer: Michael Zee
Indexer: Hilary Bird

Printed and bound in U.A.E. by Oriental Press

To find out more about our books, visit www.interlinkbooks.com and sign up for our newsletters.

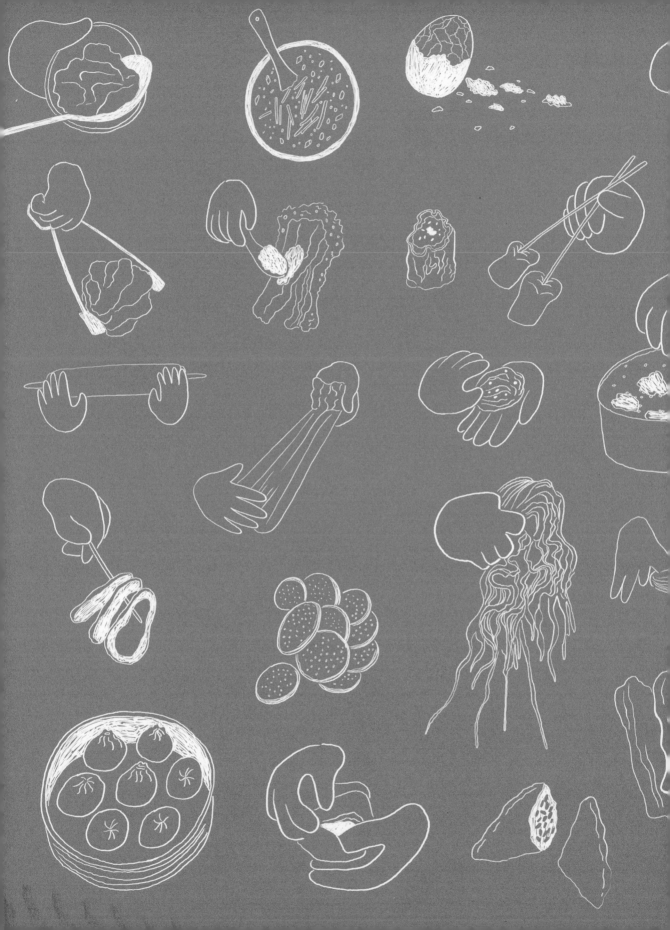